Rolando N. Grumt Suárez

111 Places in Gran Canaria That You Shouldn't Miss

111

emons:

Una escultura señera que sube del mar
tan preciosa y rica que endulza la saliva
dame un beso y otro y tres que te doy siete
soy quien soy por lo que soy, y por ti, isla de mi vida
siempre estaremos unidos, muertos o vivos
en este mundo trascendente, tú y yo, y poco más

Photographs by © Rolando N. Grumt Suárez, except:
ch. 21 (bottom): Tarek Ode; ch. 63: José Garcia;
ch. 110: AstroEduca.com
© Covermotiv: shutterstock.com/Niebieski Lew
English translation: Tom Ashforth
Layout: Eva Kraskes, based on a design
by Lübbeke | Naumann | Thoben
Maps: altancicek.design, www.altancicek.de
Basic cartographical information from Openstreetmap,
© OpenStreetMap-Mitwirkende, ODbL
Printing and binding: Grafisches Centrum Cuno, Calbe
Printed in Germany 2019
ISBN 978-3-7408-0604-0
First edition

Foreword

The Canary Islands archipelago in the eastern central Atlantic, west of Morocco and the Sahara, and more than 1,000 kilometres from the Spanish mainland, is a thunderously fluffy scattering of islands. Gran Canaria is their queen, an unimaginably grand and precious jewel on an untouched and silver-blue stretch of ocean. Having dramatically surged out of the core of mother earth in the roaring Pliocene, it is today amountainous maritime lava memorial, whose furious peak, towering over the water, is the symbol of an island kingdom so beautiful and increíble bonito. *Tocando el alma, besandoel ingenio*, finesse and serendipity hand in hand, stone for stone, invigorating the senses, immersing them in fabulous dreams *en sueños de sueños de ensueño*; blessed be the passionate life-giving wings of creativity.

Gran Canaria – a flamboyant island with irrepressible verve and an insatiable lust for life. This sparkling amalgam of nature's essence and human dissent unfurls as an aesthetically pleasing geological sculpture, drifting in the seclusion of the Atlantic, whose aura invigorates the juices of life and dreams, a colourful, sumptuous reliefon which the blossoming, flourishing and thriving of multiple forms of life forges onwards in an incomparable way. Its like may only ever be found again, with a considerable slice of luck, on some planet in a far-off galaxy. Here, on planet Earth, Gran Canaria is unrivalled – and will always remain so. This book breathes in the temperament and the glory of a boundless island, spending time in each of its 21 municipalities and revealing a mixture of known, lesser-known and unknown places, absolute sensations and symbols of the island, hidden curiosities and pearls. There is something for everyone here, no matter whether you have already visited the most beautiful island in the world or are planning a visit for the first time. *Descubre Gran Canaria*, discover Gran Canaria, *la isla de las mil maravillas*, the island of 1,000 splendours, *tan preciosa y rica que enduleza la saliva.*

111 Places

1 The Coffee Plantation

Unique beans for extraordinary coffee

There are many things on Gran Canaria that you won't find elsewhere. For example, there are quite a number of coffee plantations. We Europeans consume the black gold – though, sadly, it is no more than brown dishwater – like there's no tomorrow. And we roast coffee beans, whether by industrial methods or in a drum, for all we are worth. But we always have to import them. Not so in Valle de Agaete. No other patch of European soil, other than here in the most fertile valley on the island, offers the climatic conditions the demanding coffee tree requires.

From the highlands of Abyssinia via Arabia, Sri Lanka and Amsterdam to Agaete in the prudent hands of Santiago. His grandparents already had coffee trees in their garden for their own use. It has only been systematically and organically cultivated here since Santiago launched the project 'Café Platinium' a few years ago. The result is heavenly – Santiago's coffee is guaranteed to beguile the palate of every coffee lover. He also grows a variety of other tropical fruits between the coffee trees: papayas, guavas, prickly pears, avocados, mangos, oranges, lemons and many more.

Currently – and if he has his way it will stay so – it is Santiago himself who will lead you through this Elysian plantation, pouring out his heart in very Spanish-Spartan English. He also has a couple of words of German and Italian in his repertoire, but don't worry, no matter where you come from, you'll understand everything, despite the supposed language barrier. These warm-hearted and cheerful people still exist, burning with passion for their craft and for the chance to enable others to share in it, who, very much like the Little Prince, talk with their hearts. Those who are ready to immerse themselves sensorially in the entire variety of the valley should ask Santiago for a tour of his finca, crowned with a very fresh cup of coffee.

Address Café Platinium, Finca de Santiago Lugo, 2 Paseo de Los Romeros, 35489 El Valle de Agaete, Agaete, +34 635 510980 | **Getting there** Turn off the GC-2, through Agaete on the GC-231 and follows the signs to the finca | **Hours** Daily, summer 11am–7pm, winter 11am–5pm, price for entrance, tour and tasting €10 | **Tip** At the end of the GC-231, beyond the last town of Los Berrazales, is the mountain village of El Sao with its original houses. From the car park, follow the signs to Fagajesto and there are three ruined mills to admire. The second even has a working spring tap.

2 The E7 – Connects People

From El Hierro to the Black Sea

Ever heard of the E7? Lie group, Hubble sequence, emerging economies? Nothing of the sort! The E7 is the 7th of 12 European long-distance hiking routes and is intended to link the Atlantic with the Black Sea. It currently begins at the original ancient meridian on El Hierro and goes as far as the Romanian border. The last stretch to the Black Sea isn't marked out yet. And even though the route has already been decided, the path does not yet lead through Gran Canaria. It is supposed to go from Puerto de Las Nieves to Maspalomas. All the other islands are already on board, and Gran Canaria will soon complete the septet.

In total, the GR 131, as the long-distance trail section of the E7 on the Canary Islands is called, will be almost 600 kilometres long. The routes are marked with two horizontal lines on top of one another – the lower one is red, the one above white – painted on stones, rock faces or tree trunks. Of course, the whole thing is not everyone's cup of tea, but the planned route on Gran Canaria is in parts similar to the Camino de Santiago, i.e. the only section of the Way of St James on the Canary Islands. And walking on the Camino de Santiago is very much in at the moment.

In the summer months, it can get very hot all over the island, and the high humidity plays its part too, but the rest of the year the weather is pretty much a safe bet for crossing the island. Is there a better way to soak up Gran Canaria in all its splendour than to walk right across the island, breathing in its ambience and its magic and getting to know the people you meet along the way? And, as in every adventure, you will also get to know yourself a little better. One thing is for sure, the only true journey in life is the journey to yourself. With this in mind, the GR 131 could be an ideal way to begin or continue your journey. Off to new horizons! *¡Ampliar horizontes!*

Address GR 131 E 7, Puerto de Las Nieves, 35489 Agaete, route markings are in the making | **Getting there** From the GC-2 or the GC-200 to the GC-172, follow the signs to the harbour | **Tip** The aforementioned Camino de Santiago leads from Parroquia de Santiago de los Caballeros Gáldar via Cruz de Tejeda to the dunes of Maspalomas.

3 The Ecological Residence

Ecological, responsible habitus naturalis

Guayedra, an opulent strip of land sandwiched between Lomo del Manco and Lomo de Faneque, was the only Guanches area on the whole Canary Island archipelago that was able to negotiate an independence pact with the Castilian royal family, guaranteeing conditional sovereignty, during the Spanish conquest in the 15th century. It was indigenous leader Tenesor Semidán (c. 1447–1496) who, with great foresight, wrapped up the deal with the invaders. Tenesor spoke to the king, had himself baptised, in 1481, changed his name to Fernando Guanarteme and from then on was seen as a loyal ally of the Spanish royal family. In return, he was allowed to choose a territory. He prudently chose Guayedra and moved there with around 40 extended families. Historians term him a traitor or a negotiating genius depending on the spirit of the day.

The valley of Guayedra is formed by rugged cliff walls with imposing peaks and shallow, jagged hollows, which open out towards the sea with generous expanses. The area was neglected for decades because of disputes over ownership, but its revitalisation and reforestation has been promoted for some time. An eldorado brimming with endemic plants and animals is being woken from its deep sleep and now sparkles in blossoming splendour.

In Redondo de Guayedra, the ecological, responsible habitus naturalis is the focus. The completely refurbished finca, as well as the sports area, gym, swimming pool and bodega, all blend in with the organic garden, where dozens of fruit and vegetable varieties thrive, in an act of idyllic conformity. Furthermore, various livestock, including chickens, ducks, sheep, goats and the jenny Margarita are kept here. All of the homegrown produce finds its way into the regional-local cuisine served in the bodega. Even the honey and coffee supplied to the overnight guests here is home-produced. The Redondo is an ecological place where you can disconnect from the world.

Address Redondo de Guayedra, Barranco de Guayedra, s/n, 35489 Guayedra, Agaete, +34 928 898586, www.redondodeguayedra.com | Getting there On the GC-200 from Agaete towards La Aldea, after 5.2 kilometres follow the dirt track opposite the bus stop downhill to a large locked wooden gate with intercom | Tip The restaurant Los Almácigos de Guayedra (GC-200 at 5 kilometres), which opened in the spring of 2018, has integrated seamlessly into the ecological scene and offers its guests Canarian-fusion culinary delights in a distinguished ambience. Fancy fried Saharan squid on leaves, sprouted greens and coriander salad?

4 The Green Ray

El amor siempre gana

In matters of love it is easy to misjudge, get carried away or even be completely mistaken. I raise my hand to it. In fact, I raise two. But those who, while watching the sun set into the sea, are fortunate enough to catch a glimpse of the dazzling shimmer of the green ray, which is also known as the green light or green flash, no longer need to worry about such things as love. According to a Scottish legend, those who have seen it can no longer go wrong in love if they follow the voice of their heart. And a Gran Canarian legend goes even further: if you see it as a couple, your love will last for ever. What could go wrong?

Jules Verne built this legend as the guiding theme into his only romantic novel *Le Rayon Vert*, in which he has his romantic lead Helena search for the green ray with her two uncles Sib and Sam. On the trip they meet the nice young man Oliver, who wins Helena's affection and joins them. In the end, they manage to spot the natural physical phenomenon – as Helena and Oliver look into each other's eyes. Precisely this image found a place on the frontispiece of the book.

Éric Rohmer searched the world over for the meteorological phenomenon for the final scene of his film *Le Rayon Vert* and set up a camera in the north of Gran Canaria for an entire year in the hope of capturing it. The climatic conditions needed for a green flash are particularly common here. But Rohmer wasn't able to record a single green ray. The consequence was that he went on to create what is probably the smallest and most moving special effect in the history of film. The protagonists Delphine and Jacques experience the green ray in the finale and offer up an acting masterstroke. The chances are good on the coast of Agaete. There are several lucky devils in my circle of friends. I'm not one of them yet! But I found love nonetheless. And you? *¡Te amo mi amor!*

Address The green ray, all around the coast, for example Playa Juncal or the natural pools of Las Salinas, hills with a corresponding view of the sea | Getting there For example, the parking bays or lookouts along the GC-200, on all of Agaete's beaches or on the pier and promenade of Puerto de Las Nieves | Tip The Risco Faneque, a good view of which can be had from the harbour pier, is, at 1,027 metres, the highest cliff in Europe and the seventh highest in the world. Playa Fanque spreads out at its feet.

5_The Indigenous Beach

Chepre, Re and Atum or: sunbathers in the flow

'One Thousand and One Beaches' would be a great title for a collection of Gran Canarian stories. With over 100 beaches, the island is, in terms of its size and geological nature, one of the most 'beached' islands in the world. Here you can find the perfect beach for every kind of beach-lover. Playa de Guayedra is slightly hidden, is very quiet all year round and is well suited to the practice of nudism. Getting there requires walking quite a distance and demands a certain degree of sure-footedness.

In ancient Canarian times, this section of beach functioned as a place for rituals and ceremonies. It was their sun god that the Guanches worshipped here especially. You might assume that the round monster, sometimes smaller, sometimes larger, that descends over the horizon, taking the light with it into the bottomless pit thus making darkness the queen, was terrifying to them. But far from it! Certainly, they wouldn't want to mess with the sun god, but the sun was seen as a divine character and was revered. It was named Magec, was ascribed femininity and stood at the centre of their devotion.

The Guanches developed from a magic and cult-based civilisation to a deistic one. The solar cult, which was supplemented by a lunar one, also found its expression in cave paintings and earthenware. They revered all of the heavenly bodies, which conveyed the firmament into day or night through the course of the earth's rotation, and this found its way into every area of life. But Magec was the central element of their cosmogony, and they believed that all human souls were her daughters.

A special celebration took place on this beach every year in the early hours of the morning up to and including sunrise on 21 June. It celebrated 'the triumph of the sun'. Plant-based offerings were burned and fresh goat milk was sprayed through the air like confetti at a wedding. Hurrah!

Address Playa de Guayedra, 35489 Agaete | **Getting there** On the GC-200 from Agaete towards La Aldea after 5.2 kilometres. Follow the dirt track opposite the bus stop down towards the valley. Limited tolerated parking spaces at the right-hand bend. Follow the path on foot, walk along the side of the private plot of land towards the shore, then right to the beach. | **Tip** Playa de Sotavento is the beach's immediate neighbour and is described as *preciosa and salvaje*, glorious and wild.

6 Open-Air Water Museum

Water – yesterday's, today's and tomorrow's gold

Gran Canaria – water, water everywhere (not least in the form of the ocean all around it), but scarcely more than a drop to drink. Annual rainfall is only 300 millimetres. Granted, twice as much water falls from the heavens here than on the eastern islands, but then again it receives much less than the western islands – only about half as much as La Palma. Around 80 per cent of precipitation falls during the winter months and is limited largely to the higher altitudes. As a whole, the island lacks rainwater. This has led to the necessity of preventing water from trickling away and finding its way through the many gorges into the big drink of the Atlantic. But only around 10 per cent can actually be used – a whopping 65 per cent is already lost to evaporation.

The vast, ghostly Samsó estate and the surrounding countryside in the Tamadaba massif, contains a spectacular accumulation of human interventions, whose contemplation transforms the cultural and natural landscape into an enchanting scene, studded with hydraulic structures that offer unparalleled testimony to the history of water management on Gran Canaria. With great effort and tenacity, men and women have created structures here that enable us to understand how water was generated in centuries past. Rainwater was, is and will continue to be, worth its weight in gold.

The works of art at the Open-Air Water Museum are diverse. On one side construction debris, ruins and rubble as well as decommissioned pits and wells; on the other pipework, canals and tubes alongside dams and sluices. Then there are the ponds and pools as well as the Samsó finca with several outbuildings. A gigantic, majestic heritage treasure, flanked by hundreds of Canary Island pines, garnished with wooded views of the symbolic island peak of neighbouring Mount Teide. Take the plunge! *¡Hala, aguas a la obra!*

Address El Paisaje y Cortijo de Samsó, La Meseta y el Pinar de Tamadaba, 35489 Agaete | Getting there From the GC-210 or 217 onto the GC-216, turn right onto Camino de Los Romeros from the northerly Tamadaba ring-road to the car park. Follow the path to the right. The vast site runs along both sides of the path to the third reservoir. | Tip After a hike of several kilometres, Camino de Los Romeros ends at Plateau Era de Berbique, an ancient Canarian open-air threshing floor with an impressive lookout.

7 The Rainbow Pools

Colours give you wings in thought and feelings

Gran Canaria is the mistress of colour synthesis. There isn't a single tone or hue that can be said to be missing from its palette. Colours are nature smiling, and are perceivable as well as tangible and interpretable to us due to visible electromagnetic radiation that stimulates our retina.

Colours are acts of light, its active and passive modifications, just as the writer/statesman Johann Wolfgang von Goethe wrote all those years ago. The eye can see just as the light can see. The pools of the biosphere reserve El Risco de Agaete have made this guiding principle their own. The water shimmers iridescent on the surface, changing from one moment to the next depending on the incident of light, the strength of the sun and the play of the clouds, and celebrates a flood of hundreds of different shades. The sensual world of colours peels away the various layers of reality, existing without our calculation, purely in the orbit of our own imagination.

A path leads from El Risco, signposted to start with, through the rugged depression with its quirky stone formations and its polymorph flora to the main pool, which is fed by a 20-metre-high cascade. The route there is lined by glittering, coloured natural treasures and has one or two surprises in store for the watchful eye. Right at the main pool a geological-metaphysical phenomenon occurs that makes varied and amusing human faces appear in the random interaction of the free-falling water and the colours of the rocks.

Depending on the season and level of the pools, the waterholes can be rather inviting for bathing and for paddling. You'll often be accompanied by a songbird or two, carried away and lost in their own warbling melody.

Those who wish to bring body and psyche, heart and soul into resonance in the rush of the theory of colour, are sure to experience a multicoloured miracle in this reflective place.

Address Los Charcos Colorados, also El Charco Azul, 35489 El Risco, Agaete | Getting there GC-200 between 13 and 14 kilometres. The path through the village into open countryside is signposted 'El Charco Azul'; the pools are spread along the length of the path and guide your way. | Tip To the right of the main pool you can go further up, but off the beaten track, towards a double waterfall, which almost steals the Charco Azul show when the volume of water is great enough.

8 The Abandoned Bunker

Not quite legal, not quite regal

General Francisco Franco came out of the Spanish Civil War as the victor. He turned the Republic of Spain into a dictatorship that lasted until 1975. In 1940, Adolf Hitler negotiated with his Spanish counterpart over Spain's entry into World War II. Franco placed high demands, but Hitler did not accept them. The Führer tried again later, but Franco insisted on his conditions. A historic tragedy in two respects: if Spain had entered into the war, Franco's days would have been numbered, at the very latest by 1945, and the country would have been spared the rest of his bloody dictatorship. On the other hand, it would have played an even more inglorious role in the history of the world war.

The Germans and the British played cat and mouse on the Canary Islands during World War II, using the archipelago as an important strategic location. But the Germans had an advantage: Franco gave them carte blanche to use all Spanish harbours and airports. Spain became a backyard for the Nazi regime, but on the Canary Islands, however, the British held the upper hand. Nonetheless, the Wörmann high-rise in Las Palmas, now luxuriously modernised, for example, functioned as the coordination headquarters for German secret agents, and numerous military bunkers and munitions depots were erected.

The abandoned military bunker in Arinaga is an important witness to these involvements. It is shrouded in many myths. They run the entire gambit, from paranormal activity via pagan and satanic rituals, corpses and carcasses to the ghostly apparitions of former soldiers. Locked gates at the main entrances are no obstacle to adrenalin junkies. But be careful, both in the bunker itself as well as on the way there. The occasional homeless person lives wild on Montaña de Arinaga, sheltering in cave-like dwellings. They have a tendency to react badly to strangers.

Address Batería Militar de Arinaga, Montaña de Arinaga, s/n, 35118 Arinaga, Agüimes | Getting there From the GC-1 on to the GC-100 towards Arinaga, left onto Calle Almirante Arriaga just before the village, then right onto Calle García de Toledo and left on Paseo del Faro. Montaña de Arinaga rises up on the left side and the bunker is to be found on its southeastern flank. | Tip Opposite, a few hundred metres as the crow flies, is Faro de Arinaga, the lighthouse. Since the summer of 2016 it has been the home of a restaurant serving Canarian-Mediterranean food. It is also possible to visit the dome.

9_The Bustling Sculpture Location

Unscrupulous sculptures scalp scabby skinks

Scabby skinks scalp unscrupulous sculptures. Or something like that. Either way, the town of Agüimes is an eldorado for sculpture. Although, it should really just be Dorado. Eldorado suffered the same fate as alcohol. In the Arabic al-kuhl, the al is only, like the el in the Spanish el dorado, the article to the noun. Merged together they form a cheeky neologism – how and why isn't actually all that important to our story.

On every corner, on every roundabout, in every alleyway and probably under every top hat too – this town certainly won't sink into oblivion due to a lack of sculptures. The townsfolk of Agüimes are infatuated with their sculptures, and new ones are added to the collection almost every week. There certainly seems to be enough space; after all, they see the sculptures as beautification of their town, and so space is found even on private land for their installation. Furthermore, it all happens within the framework of the project 'Agüimes, un museo al aire libre', which means, roughly translated, 'Agüimes, a museum in the open air'.

Los Enamorados is an extremely popular sculpture by Ana Luisa Benítez on Callejón el Reloj, an alleyway that connects Calle el Sol and Calle el Progreso. Apart from 'The Lovers', there are several other sculptures by the versatile Gran Canarian artist in Agüimes. Benítez is seen as one of the most distinguished of her genre.

El Futuro es Mujer is an inconspicuous but emblematic sculpture by Francisco Suárez Díaz and is located on the way out of town, directly on Avenida la Salle, which is simultaneously the GC-100. 'The Future Is Woman' is from 1998, and its symbolism is now, in these times of gender equality, quotas for women, the Me Too debate and the Eurovision Song Contest winner Netta, more topical than ever.

Address Los Enamorados, Callejón el Reloj, s/n, between Calle el Sol and Calle el Progreso, 35260 Agüimes; El Futuro es Mujer, Avenida la Salle, s/n, on the corner of Calle Juan Ramon Jimenez, 35260 Agüimes | Tip The restaurant Alpendre del Artet is at 42 Calle Dr Joaquín Artiles. Snail stew, grilled pepper salad with tuna, fresh fish, several varieties of barbecued meat, accompanied by a prickly pear fruit cocktail. Hungry?

10_Canary Gold

In the heart of a volcano, on the tongue of a poem

Rhodium is the most expensive and speculative precious metal on earth, but it will never reach the symbolic power of gold in terms of wealth, preciousness and exquisiteness. And this is also why gold, and no other metal, is often used as a lexicalised metaphor. There is black gold, meaning, depending on the season, crude oil, truffles or caviar; white gold, which is sugar (actually white poison), marble or salt, and then there's Canary gold alias olive oil from the Canary Islands.

Treated shabbily for a long time, Canarian olive oil production has experienced a veritable boom in recent years, just like aloe vera and wine production. In this globalised era of cost-efficient mass production, home-grown produce is in greater demand than ever before, and so quite a few families and companies here have also shifted their focus to regional ecological agriculture. Due to other monocultures and mass tourism, some of the island's olive groves have lain fallow for many years, until now, as the generations move on, the young return to their grandparents' fields and revive the centuries-old olive oil tradition using up-to-date agricultural methods.

The family of mother Rita and son Manuel started their olive oil project a good 10 years ago and now count themselves among the award-winning olive oil producers on the island. Olives are collected by hand and pressed on the same day. Their *almazara*, as the pressing plants are called in Spanish (and 'mill' in English), including one of the island's oldest olive groves with unbelievable views, is located in a small, secluded hamlet in the middle altitudes of the southeast of the island. On a guided tour through the grove and site here they will insist that you pour some of the gently cold-pressed Canary gold, with its roots in this volcanic earth, down your throat to achieve smooth saliva symbiosis. Gold nectar!

Address Almazara Oro Canario, Lomo de la Cruz, s/n, 35118 Agüimes, +34 669346219, info@orocanario.com | **Getting there** On the GC-551 between 4 and 5 kilometres on the GC-815, take the steep off-road track to the right at the sharp left at Camping de Temisas. The gate is around 100 metres on. | **Hours** Viewing and tours can be arranged by phone or email | **Tip** The Temisas campsite offers a homely family atmosphere, which Doña Carmen, the hostess and good-hearted soul, values highly.

11 The Charming Cheese Dairy

Nannies, rams, bucks and a couple of kids

Two yellowing signs written in many languages, one on the nearest crossing, one directly in the yard, indicate that there's a dairy here. And indeed, even though the farm appears anything but inviting and seems almost abandoned, goat cheese is still made here on a small scale according to family tradition. The signs are left over from times gone by, when the now older generation used to sell straight from the farm. Which the current generation does too, but no longer primarily to passing trade. If a wanderer does occasionally happen to stray here, it is more likely that they were following their intuition rather than purposefully seeking out the dairy. The cheese is actually sold to local cheese epicureans or directly to cheese dealers.

The first time I was here, my father brought me. It must be at least 20 years ago. One thing certainly hasn't changed: now, as back then, this cheese tastes outstanding. When I last visited to buy some, I was welcomed by the cleaning lady, who first indulged me with a cheese feast. Very rudimentary, very uncomplicated and very much without any chichi, jiggery-pokery or knick-knacks, but instead lots of chit-chat. Heavenly! They produce semi-hard and hard cheeses with various rinds. Excellent!

As Gustave Flaubert once said: 'A dinner which ends without cheese is like a beautiful woman with only one eye.' Pungent! By the way, you won't find any individually packed hunks of cheese here. In general the cheese, some of which is award-winning, leaves the farm by the wheel. But as a rule there are usually one or two open wheels, from which they are happy to cut you a piece. The farm is a working home. You won't find any pomp and circumstance here, just a small cold store, a couple of implements and of course loads of nannies, rams, bucks and kids. This place is all about the cheese.

Address Quesería La Era del Cardón, GC-551, s/n, 35270 Agüimes | **Getting there** On the GC-551 between 6 and 7 kilometres | **Hours** No regular times, but most customers come in the morning | **Tip** On the GC-551, at the crossroad with the GC-65, are the ruins of a building with cave elements. With a bit of luck you might find an opal or an olivine, which the area is well known for and which used to be made into jewellery in this complex of buildings.

12_The Colossal Gorge

Sobbing with joy, overwhelmed by beauty

Gran Canaria is the island of gorges. There seems to be a gorge lurking around every corner. There isn't even an official number – but there are hundreds, if not thousands. Gorges belong to the island's most striking, differentiated traits and represent its most important geomorphological peculiarity. These unique realms form unspoiled ecosystems that enjoy rich biodiversity, in which a largely indigenous flora prevails and numerous Canarian and Moroccan endemic species are to be found – from euphorbias and cactuses to the Gran Canaria giant lizard and a unique species of bat. In the past, they offered early settlers shelter; today they are nature refuges or serve the flourishing of natural agricultural produce. But they are predominantly left to themselves and are protected nature conservation areas.

Nonetheless, they haven't all remained untouched. Some have even been built on. Such is the case in the colossal gorge of Guayadeque, one of the largest on the island with an area of 743.7 hectares. There are a couple of small inhabited zones, pre-hispanic troglodytic cave colonisations, Guanches burial sites and storage caves, in which mummies covered in skin were found, a neat chapel, some ruins, several cafés, restaurants and accommodation facilities and, of course, the very wide road, which runs right through the valley, curving slightly for a couple of kilometres.

The well-developed gorge is a popular destination because of its commercial and cultural use, both among locals as well as visitors.

'Guayadeque' is a Guanches word, probably of African origin. The Canary Islands belong, topographically, to Africa, and although the origin of the Guanches, the aboriginal Canarians, has not been conclusively determined, one theory suggests that they descended from Saharan desert dwellers. The African prefix 'Wua' equates to 'Gua'.

Address Barranco de Guayadeque, 35260 Agüimes, the whole of the GC-103 from around 1.5 kilometres | **Getting there** From the GC-100 to the north of Agüimes onto Calle la Orilla, the GC-103 | **Tip** The Guayadeque Interpretation Centre, directly on the GC-103, presents the history of the gorge and prehistoric art.

13 El Cabrón Diving Area

The spirit must dive often to avoid capsizing

'Errors, like straws, upon the surface flow; He who would search for pearls, must dive below' – the English poet John Dryden (1631 – 1700) giving it his all back in the day. Experienced divers know about the pearliness of the marine reserve El Cabrón, which means 'the ram', or, if we're being strictly accurate, the billy goat. Although some would now raise an index finger and wish to make you aware of another meaning. Yes, the word cabrón is often used in Spain and can be translated as either son of a gun, dirty pig or asshole. In general, however, it is suitable for daily use, mostly meant with a nod and a wink, and rarely as a nasty insult.

El Cabrón offers a complex submarine ecosystem, made up of caves, caverns, reefs, bizarre rock formations, drop-offs, openings, arches and deep-blue water. You can see a variety of sea creatures, including barracudas, stingrays, angel sharks, seahorses and squids. A volcanic underwater landscape, which is considered by connoisseurs as one of the best diving areas in the archipelago.

A handful of diving schools are based in Arinaga, both PADI certified as well as hipper versions, which also offer the ultimate in underwater fun: scooters. The torpedo-shaped mobility aid, which was developed with the substantial involvement of the diving legend Jacques-Yves Cousteau, is not just an amusing gimmick, but in fact an extremely useful device designed with technical finesse. Underwater scooters extend the possible radius of action, and with a perfectly primed scooter and the corresponding handling you can greatly expand your diving possibilities.

Gran Canaria's annual underwater photography contests such as 'Fotosub Las Palmas' or 'The Canary Islands Dive Photo Challenge' are also extremely popular. The photos, from the spectacular to the breathtaking, are shown as part of an exhibition or presented online.

Address La Reserva Marina del Cabrón, 35118 Arinaga, Agüimes | **Getting there** From the GC-1 onto the GC-100 towards Arinaga, left into Calle Almirante Arriaga just before the town, then right into Calle García de Toledo and left onto Paseo del Faro. Follow it to the end and instead of turning right to the lighthouse, go straight on along the gravel path to the Playa del Cabrón beach. Access in full gear from the beach. | **Tip** Another fascinating diving spot, 'La Catedral', is northeast of Las Palmas. It's a spectacular submarine labyrinth in a rocky massif at a depth of between 6 and 40 metres. Only accessible by boat.

14 The First-Class Surfing Spot

Everybody's gone surfin', surfin' Gran Canaria

Brian Wilson of the Beach Boys actually forgot to integrate a surfing spot on Gran Canaria into the lyrics of the semi-plagiarised song 'Surfin' U.S.A.'. He knew no better, so he's forgiven. Playa de Vargas is definitively one of the most attractive surfing spots on the island and is trisected by imaginary lines running out into the sea: the northern part is reserved for bathers, the middle section for windsurfers and the southern part for kitesurfers. People hardly ever get in each other's way, even if Juanmi, one of my good resident friends, always complains that many visitors, and even locals, completely ignore the rules.

Juanmi has a WhatsApp group together with other surf buddies, in which the most important info does the rounds on a daily basis. There is always someone looking for the best conditions, so they exchange tips among themselves and know over the course of the morning which surfing spot on the island has the best waves or where the wind is most favourable. It is often here!

Playa de Vargas is spoiled for wind all year round. In the winter months and right into spring, the spot is seen as one of the best, but even in the summer months it can hold a candle (though it would literally be impossible to keep it alight) to Gran Canaria's much better known surfing spot, Pozo Izquierdo (see ch. 79). At high tide the place is wild, and there are lots of shorebreaks. Generally suitable for all levels of proficiency, experience is required on the rougher days.

Have you ever heard the name Philip Köster? Born in Las Palmas de Gran Canaria and brought up on Playa de Vargas as the child of surfing teachers from Hamburg, Philip is the first German and second-youngest windsurfing world champion in the 'wave riding' discipline. With a bit of luck you could be sharing the waves with him. Surfomania!

Address Playa de Vargas, 35269 Vargas, Agüimes | Getting there From the GC-1 onto the GC-100 towards Cruze de Arinaga, then on the GC-191, westwards parallel to the GC-1, towards Playa de Vargas, turn onto the GC-2-6 and follow the signs | Tip The campsite Vargas with restaurant, caravan/camper van area, tent site, wooden chalets and barbecues is one of the largest on the island and isn't reserved just for surfers. PS: Sorry, no, Juanmi didn't give me permission to publish his number.

15_The Heaving Summer Bar

Sit, smile, stare and sensibly do nothing

This small unobtrusive summer bar on Muelle de Arinaga creates a furore each year. Summer bar, because it only opens its doors during the summer months. Local heroes and island dwellers gather in front of and around the bar in droves, creating an idle ambience by hanging around and watching the world go by. On a summer's day, without the stress of appointments and with your cares packed securely away, there is nothing better than giving yourself over to the sounds, sights and sensations. The sounds of the sea and the buzz of the people, the sight of the sun on the water, and the feeling of the sun on your skin, and, should you choose, of alcohol in your bloodstream. Meaningfully idling – you really don't need much more to celebrate moments of happiness.

Typical Canarian dishes are prepared in the small kitchen. The real punters' favourite is 'Sancocho de cherne', a wreckfish dish with potato, sweet potato and dumplings made from that Canarian staple, gofio. Elsewhere it can be quite bland, but the locals swear by the version served here, prepared to a recipe passed down through generations. Among those in the know, the bar is also called 'El Bar del Sancocho'. The insider tip is the 'Ensalada Charquito'.

The pub was originally called 'Bar de Catalinita'. Opened around 1940 by Catalina, it was the first on Arinaga beach. It has been family owned since then, and the building has hardly changed, apart from a spot of paint on the façade and some maintenance work. To all intents and purposes, it is a small residential house, that once served a double function.

The pub is furnished with shelves and a bar. Framed photos of old Arinaga hang on the walls. The staff will serve anyone who is in sight, with or without a seat, with or without their wallet drawn, sitting, standing or swimming. The latter are delivered their order on a converted remote-controlled model boat.

Address Bar Universidad, 2 Avenida del Molino, 35118 Arinaga, Agüimes | **Getting there** From the GC-1 onto the GC-100 towards Arinaga, through the town on Avenida Polizón, right at the roundabout. On foot, on the right-hand side after 50 metres. | **Hours** May–Sept Sat & Sun, from late morning to late in the evening | **Tip** Playa de Arinaga and the pier have morphed into a popular sunbathing hideaway in recent years. Soak up the sun! Build sandcastles! Listen to the sea!

16 The Maritime Moon Path

There are many promenades, few are magical

The sky is clear, the stars bright. It is midnight and the moon awakens. The Magec (i.e. the sun, see ch. 5) has disappeared and yet she is the biggest light. The waves break, one on top of the other, to a crashing crescendo. Finally, it is the darkness that reigns. With neither fright nor fear, but in fact quite uninhibited. Only thoughts carry you, step by step. The spirit in freedom, undisturbed and in happy melancholy. They exist, these moments of being at one with the earth, in harmony. A calm, contemplative stroll instead of an excited, wild ride. A feeling like gentle butterflies in the rush of love. Or teenagers with a lust for life.

On a warm summer evening or a heavenly night, this beach promenade has many aces up its sleeve. Put your arm around your dearest Tom, Dick or Harry, or Kate, Anne or Jane and saunter back and forth for a while at your leisure. And treat yourself to a culinary pleasure, be it liquid or solid, in one of the restaurants or bars. But beware of the cockroaches! These creatures wake in the small hours, and there is no worse scourge. And remember – the night owl catches the beetle.

Tomorrow's dinner swims in the ocean; the bigger the sea, the more you see. The salt in the air shapes the character of those who live on the land, so characteristically gentle and wild at the same time. Coastal birds with and without wings, but always on two legs, let themselves be led by the capricious atmosphere. Like driftwood in the dance of the molecules, the atoms and quantums take each other by the hand.

The immediate surroundings merge with the horizon. Magic moments of breathing, listening and feeling. A place to linger. A place of contemplative time. Time stands still. No clock, only the silence ticks. If you don't dream here, then you've forgotten how to dream, but you will soon learn again. *¡Vivir es soñar!*

Address Paseo Marítimo de Arinaga, 35118 Arinaga, Agüimes, from the southernmost part of the promenade via the pier to Punta del Mato (to the lighthouse) | Getting there From the GC-1 to the GC-100 towards Arinaga, turn right onto Calle Almirante Arriaga just before the town, then left onto Calle Magallanes. The first section of the promenade is at the end of the road. | Tip Bar Ca' Beli on Avenida Polizón in the middle of the traffic-calmed pedestrian zone parallel to the pier makes homemade stews to die for and still serves drinks and snacks at the witching hour.

17_The Mystical Ghost House

The blurring of reality, dreams and magic

If one doesn't take care of things in life, neglect sneaks in, and things start to take their own course – towards an uncertain conclusion. That is what happened to this architectural treat, which has been nibbled at by the teeth or to be more accurate the whole jaw of time. But also by the teeth of ghosts, angels and demons, who are all, apparently, housemates here.

At first glance, the house has got nothing to do with Isabel Allende's *The House of the Spirits*, the book that was made into a film by Bille August starring, among others, Meryl Streep, Winona Ryder, Glenn Close, Jeremy Irons and Antonio Banderas. But it does if you take a closer look, as Allende's debut novel, a Chilean family chronicle, written with abundant affection, is peppered with magical-mystical characteristics. The house certainly scores big in the fairytale stakes.

At some point in the past, the building was used as a museum and arts and crafts studio, and was open to the general public. A yellowing sign on the road points vaguely to former, more stately times. In wistful daydreaming, you can catapult yourself back to that glamorous era and get an inkling of how vibrant and lively it must have once been here. But today spiritism, angelology and demonology have taken over. Ghosts, angels and demons, it would seem, all do their thing here, until the beams creak and bend and become ghosts themselves. There is a rumour doing the rounds that a group of kindred spirits regularly gathers in the house in order to pursue spiritualist activities.

This place is steeped in a special aura and radiates a particular energy. You can walk all around it. At the back there is an open, overgrown back door. In many places nature merges with the mystical ghost house. A truly meta-mystical transcendental occult house, that is sure to send a shiver down any spine. And for some, right through the stomach too.

Address La Casa de Los Espíritus, originally Museo y Artesanía El Molino, GC-191, s/n, 1 Calle Mozart, 35118 Las Rosas, Agüimes | Getting there From the GC-1 onto the GC-100 towards Cruze de Arinaga, further on the GC-191, westwards parallel to the GC-1, the house is right on the GC-191 at the extended corner of Calle Mozart. | Tip Las Rosas is to be found on the GC-191, at 1 Calle Granados. A typical spartan Canarian, or is it Canarian spartan, dive. They serve soups, sandwiches and barbecue offerings.

18_The Spectacular Caves

A foundling in the care of a giant

A giant, a bat and a human child – sounds like all the ingredients needed for a mysterious fable. According to the story, the giant Gigamonomagig, who was from Rome, was woken in his cave by the crying of a child. The sound came from the ensemble of caves on the other side of the gorge, which served predominantly as a granary, but also had sleeping hollows and a crypt area.

Gigamonomagig wanted to check on the child, but the entrance to the cave was too small for him. The muscular bat Manam came to his aid, carrying the child over to him without further ado. It was wearing an armband on which the name 'Anna' was written. The next day, and the following days too, there was no trace of the parents. It became clear to Gigamonomagig that the child had been abandoned, and so the human child grew up with him from then on.

The fable stands for brotherly love between all the creatures of the cosmos. Those who visit both caves, one after the other, are bewitched by a love spell if they belt out the following five times in a row, forwards and backwards, from the cave, into the gorge: 'AMOR VALE ANNA ELAV ROMA'.

The 'Cuevas del Pósito', also known incorrectly as 'Cuevas de La Audiencia' and strictly speaking (among Temisas locals) as 'Cuevas del Risco Pintado', are reached via a path that turns off 50 metres before the bus stop on the GC-550 at around 9 kilometres opposite the Calle los Blanquiazules to 'La Inmaculada' (parking right at the beginning). The entrance to the cave can be tricky to find, but it's worth the effort: a long, narrow, but accessible entrance tunnel, two caves connected by columns and over 20 different sized holes, in other words silos. The 'Cueva del Gigante' is just as spectacular, without silos, but with a number of complex chambers. The entrance is equally inconspicuous at first, but smaller and narrower, and requires scrambling through.

Address Cuevas del Risco Pintado and Cueva del Gigante, GC-550, s/n, 35280 Temisas, Agüimes | Getting there Cuevas del Risco Pintado: GC-550, after 9 kilometres follow the path near the bus stop, right and upwards at the fork, then continue centrally to the entrance around 100 metres away; Cueva del Gigante: GC-550, after 6.5 kilometres, right past the observatory, on the left side after around 100 metres. | Tip In the hamlet of Temisas you will find the Piscina Municipal, the municipal open-air swimming pool with an amphitheatre flair. Only open in summer.

19_The Stone Toboggan Run

Not long, but striking and brilliant

Here is a hidden geological treasure that seems like a miniature example when compared with its relatives, like Jordan's Wadi Rum or the Wadi Bani Khalid in Oman. This wadi only stretches to a length of just less than 100 metres, yet it knows just how to enchant visitors with its captivating form: a creative-artistic mini canyon formed by water over the course of the millennia, which can easily hold its own alongside the paintings of Pablo Picasso. Whimsically picturesque, the canyon triggers a firework of emotions, as if magical energy seduces the atmosphere to dance.

When you're standing in the middle of it, you either feel as though you're in a stone toboggan run or on some other planet. But don't you feel something completely different now and then? In the right light, with smartly chosen framing, you can create very surreal photos, which leads us right back to Picasso. But just look, don't touch! At least don't write or draw on the walls and don't dent or damage them. Unfortunately, this is precisely what some cabrónes (see ch. 13), in the most literal sense, did at the start of 2018: writing and scratching along the walls of the wadi! As if this precious treasure was the inner wall of a train station toilet cubicle. After such vandalism, well-known mountain guides and conservationists from across the archipelago are now demanding protection for the wadi.

From time to time, look up towards the sky. It is highly likely that you are being watched. No, not primarily by a drone or a satellite, rather by a *Calandrella rufescens*, generally known as the lesser short-toed lark. If this songbird should happen to be in the mood, usually while circling or rising up in a spiral, then listen carefully to your voyeur. But don't bear any sort of grudge against this little bird, otherwise it may take revenge with a serious load of natural fertiliser.

Address Tobas de Colores del Barranco de Barafonso, also Barranco de Las Vacas, 35270 Agüimes | Getting there GC-550, after 15 kilometres (one solitary unofficial parking space available) cross the crash barrier before the bridge (southeast), follow the path downwards and walk through the bridge tunnel | Tip The dwarf wadi is flanked by Lomo del Peladero and Seto del Capitán, which can be ascended with the right climbing gear. Down by the tunnel, in the opposite direction, after around 200 metres, are the ruins of an 18th-century stone bridge. A legend says that those who hop over it on one foot will make real fools of themselves.

20_The Cave Chapel

Pilgrimage to God's grotto

Making pilgrimages isn't going to go out of fashion any time soon. People are following the holy routes like there's no tomorrow, often capturing their exploits in self-created snapshots and Madonna poses, which are studiously commented on in virtual circles and are tagged with a thumbs up and a halo. Of course, there are several holy pilgrim paths on Gran Canaria. The truest is the Camino de Santiago, which I have already mentioned when introducing the people-uniting E7 (see ch. 2). However, it will not lead you through the village of Artenara, unless you can be persuaded to leave the path. God surely wouldn't mind, after all you'll be wanting to visit the Ermita la Virgen de la Cuevita, one of the island's most sacred houses of God, which scores especially highly with its symbiosis of simplicity and beauty and the special location and form of its construction.

At 1,270 metres above sea level, Artenara is the highest village on the island and has had to win the affection of visitors over the years. Not so surprising, as the meandering journey up here, high up in the middle of nowhere, but still the beating heart of the island, is arduous and energy sapping. In the meantime, the village has adjusted to the appearance of new arrivals and there is even free WiFi in one or two places.

The year 2018 began in wintery fashion on Gran Canaria and some big storms raged (yes, there was even snow in the mountains), which caused a lot of damage in some places. One of these places was on the GC-210, the main southern access road to Artenara, where a landslide destabilised several tonnes of material and swept along a good 25-metre section of the asphalted mountain road with it. Happily for us, the authorities have finally got around to repairing the road. So nothing should stand in the way of a visit to the chapel. Don't forget your halo!

Address Ermita la Virgen de La Cuevita, 50 Calle de la Cuevita, 35350 Artenara | **Getting there** In Artenara, over Plaza San Matías turn into Calle de la Cuevita. The chapel is at the end of the road. | **Hours** Daily 9am–7pm | **Tip** The annual festival honouring the Virgen de la Cuevita takes place on the last Sunday in August. Here you can tank up on sincere devotion, er, celebrate your faith.

21 The Genuine Temple Caves

Archaeological, architectural and astronomical

The cosmos, the entirety of space, time and all the material and energy in it, whether thought of as a plasma universe, a multidimensional universe or as created by the Big Bang, is a fascination for every earthling. The universe is so unimaginably large and nebulous and the earth, including humanity, so unimaginably small and perplexing (and silly), it's easy for an earthling to lose their mind. Or to give themselves over to the demonic hands of illusionary god-like figures.

How – in god's name – was it possible that an island people, isolated from the rest of the world, such as the Guanches, had the astronomical knowledge that enabled them to control both sunlight and moonlight, in order to direct it into a temple cave and transform it into an artificial annual calendar, that shows both equinoxes and both solstices respectively? The sunlight penetrates into the cave from March to October, while in the rest of the year the moonlight does its job.

Risco Maldito or Risco Caído, a troglodytic settlement with 21 caves discovered in 1996, is second to none on any other of the 100,000-plus of our planet's islands. The unique character of this astro-archaeological, architectural-matriarchal heritage site is unparalleled. The largest collection of triangular symbol cave paintings is also to be found here. El Paisaje Cultural de Risco Caído y los Espacios Sagrados de Montaña, so the whole cultural landscape, which includes Caldera de Tejeda, the Tamadaba massif and parts of Barranco Hondo, has been nominated for the list of UNESCO World Heritage Sites.

This valuable historical treasure was a very sacred place for the Guanches, in which they connected with their gods. Whether these gods were gods in the actual sense or extraterrestrial, maybe multidimensional beings who communicated via the laws of resonance, remains written in the stars.

Address Yacimiento Arqueológico y Conjunto Sagrado Risco Caído, GC-217, s/n, 35350 Artenara, visitas.grancanariapatrimonio.com | Getting there On the C-217, take the off-road track at the most easterly point of Presa de Los Pérez, before the bridge, and then follow the signs on foot | Hours Caves can only be visited on a reserved tour with organised arrival and departure times, as spaces are extremely limited. Further information and reservations online. | Tip Walk across the Presa de Los Pérez dam, which leads into an enchanted forest.

22 The Progressive Blocks

Anti-corrosive tribute to nature and environment

As if Máximo Riol Cimas had nailed the German philosopher Martin Heidegger's phrase 'In the work of art the truth of an entity has set itself to work' like a flag to the mast, the Spanish-Canarian sculptor is constantly searching for the truth in his works of art. The artist also searches for origin, representing it himself, but also having his origin represented in the work, as one does not exist without the other – they both have their origin in art after all. Art: a truly eternal riddle.

The airy futuristic blocks made of COR-TEN steel – one standing, the other lying – are placed in a prominent location, on a splendid viewing platform in this bucolic village, the highest on the island, an entwined patch of earth in the middle of the island. They bear the title Monumento a los Trabajadores de Medio Ambiente y Conversacion (Monument to the Environment and Nature Conservation Workers). Light and easy, airy and flaky, this piece of art could also be by Eduardo Chillida – he also works with large, imposing sculptures. Emptiness as a space to be filled, as a unique vision of a vacuum and as the portrayal of another dimension. Rather like a film negative that inspires us to unnatural interpretations of reality.

The vertical object reflects cave genesis in its symbolic reference to the troglodytic dwellings, while the cylindrical stalks – meaning the long, thin pipes and not the delicate long-legged baby-bringing bird, which you may see in the wild here if you're lucky (i.e. storks) – are supposed to imitate the trunks of pine trees and stand for the Canarian forest.

The horizontal object allegorises the primal, wild and untameable landscape scenery of this mountainous region, linked with the daydream aspiration that future generations may develop a little more humility towards the beneficial kingdom of nature. Sadly, this is usually not the case!

Address El Mirador de la Atalaya, 27 Avenida Matías Vega, 35350 Artenara | Getting there Cross through the village northwards on the GC-21 and you will see it on the left at the end of the village | Tip A few hundred metres further south as the crow flies is a five-metre-tall figure of Christ, designed by José Luis Marrero Cabrera, the little brother of Cristo Redentor from Rio de Janeiro so to speak. In 1990, the then priest of Artenara, Domingo Báez González, won the equivalent of €3,000 on the lottery and without further ado invested the winnings in the acquisition of this likeness of Christ.

23 The Flanking Tower

Across from the flank, onto the head and GOOOAL!

Football, football and even more football. Since the 2017/18 season, the football has no longer been top tier on Gran Canaria, but there are hundreds, nay thousands, of football pitches and other places used for ballet with a ball, spread over the whole island. Football is the sport on Gran Canaria, even if the same can be said for many other places on earth. Too many? Football will suffer a crash, at the very latest when Lionel Messi, the best player of all time by miles, stops playing. Outrageous theory? It's true.

At any rate, the children of San Andrés continue to chase the dream of becoming a world star of football. They like to gather on the newly designed plaza in front of the church for a kickabout, no matter the weather. We clearly aren't talking about chess on grass. First of all, the plaza isn't covered in artificial turf, and second the kids know about as much about tactical trickery as novice gag writers know about humour. I include myself in there! No matter, for as Friedrich Wilhelm Nietzsche once said: 'Understanding the depth of the world means understanding the contradiction.'

The flanking tower is the only remnant of a former fortress. It is a charming piece of history that is hardly noticed any more. Not even the inhabitants of San Andrés know quite what it's doing, or did, there. Asking questions about its biography leads to shoulder shrugging.

Only Paco, a pensioner armed with a walking stick, had anything to say about the tower. He also didn't really know exactly how the story of the tower goes, but he uses a large hole inside it as a rubbish bin. He collects the rubbish lying around the place and carries it to the tower. There are real bins too, I interject. He's been doing it like that for years, so there's no use some greenhorn like me coming along, trying to be a smart alec. Will that be all? Paco, a very charming man!

Address El Torreón de San Andrés, Plaza San Andrés, 35414 San Andrés, Arucas | **Getting there** On the GC-2 Las Palmas towards Agaete, right after the second zebra crossing in San Andrés. The tower is in the northwestern corner of the plaza. | **Tip** If you walk through the flanking tower, which, if you do it several times a day, brings beauty and health (according to Paco), and follow the path to the right and down to the sea, you will find 'La Casa de los Mil Azulejos', a house with 1,000 tiles on its façade, on the left.

24 The Forest of Ropes

Living your Tarzan dreams in a gripping setting

We recently visited Gran Canaria's first and only high rope course with our children and we all had terrific fun. The children ran around on the rope bridges and hanging bridges, swinging from platform to platform, climbing up and down metre-high nets, strapping on their harnesses and flying across the abyss again and again on the Flying Fox – a 120-metre zip wire. Oh, how happy and high-spirited the kids were. And they fell asleep as soon as we got into the car to drive home. High five!

Apropos high wire, the Swiss author Markus Weidmann once said: 'The truth is a tightrope, swaying in the stormy winds of human weakness. And sadly so very near to supposed safe ground: the deceptive swamps and quicksand of lies.' We felt that this was a little too profound for the children, so we decided to chat about the really important issues in life: ice cream, ice cream and ice cream again. High five!

And as if the rope course were not already exciting enough, there is also a paintball area. At first the children didn't even realise it was there, and we acted as innocently as the pope, but it was clear that it was only a matter of time until they discovered it. And discover it they did, right after the first round of climbing, as the panoramic view from up there is excellent. And the view on top of that – simply amazing. We wanted a piece of it too! But it isn't so easy, as age certainly plays its role, and you also need a group to play with. It is mainly groups of young people or adults, who reserve in advance – a paintball fight rarely comes about spontaneously. But luck played into our hands. A children's birthday party had reserved and still had some places free in their teams. High five!

In bed, later in the evening, all cosy, cuddly and tucked up, we counted our high-five moments: a total of three! That's our record for a day. High five!

Address Parque GrancAventura, Lugar Vasco López, s/n, 35400 Arucas, +34 928 936393, www.grancaventura.com | **Getting there** From the GC-20 on Lugar Vasco López, follow the signs | **Hours** Sat, Sun & holidays 11am–8pm, Mon–Fri only with reservation | **Tip** A stone's throw away, though maybe quite a powerful one (five minutes' drive), is the restaurant Irejul, which is part of the Hotel Melva Suite. Seasonal produce from their own vegetable gardens are prepared in a Canarian-Mediterranean style and presented and plated beautifully. *¡Buen provecho!*

25__The Natural Pools

Canarian Kneipp cure on the lively rocky coast

Kneipp like a Canary? In rainwater or seawater? Your wish is this island's command! There are natural and partially prepared pools all over Gran Canaria that promise bathing with a kick. I have picked out three natural baths fed by the Atlantic that can all be visited within a single day trip. It doesn't always have to be a binary choice between the chlorine-heavy hotel pool or the roaring open ocean. But if you're not prepared to leave your comfort zone: tough luck!

'Los Charcones' in Arucas are three largely shallow pools with sandy and stony beds, the walls of which are partially furnished with non-slip mats. There are plenty of terraces for sunbathing, as well as restaurants and a number of bathrooms.

'Roque Prieto' in Santa María de Guía are two rock pools of varying depths with constantly changing crystal-clear water, which allows a fantastic view of the rocky bottom. It is a perfect place for carefree swimming.

'Las Salinas' in Agaete are several autonomously fed, connected sea pools in miniature medieval fortress style, with a stone sun deck and twisting underwater lava tunnels.

All natural pools fill up to the rhythm of the tides and should be enjoyed with caution in stormy, high-tide phases. The Canary Islands Kneipp cure enjoys great popularity and has a long tradition. Even the Guanches practised this kind of bathing. They also created rainwater-fed pools in rocky caves, which can only be imagined today, since they hardly fill up with water any more. Some of these pools are also hard to get to, requiring long walks through open terrain.

Most of the 20-plus sea pools on Gran Canaria, on the other hand, are easily accessible. The contrast to the fun of the sea to be had at the beach is clear – the natural pools all have their own, very unique charm and delight the senses. If only Sebastian Anton Kneipp had known about these natural pools!

Getting there Los Charcones: on the GC-2 Las Palmas towards Agaete, turn off at Vía de servicio (service exit), then turn off at El Puertillo. The pools are on the most northwesterly part of Paseo Maritimo los Charcones. Roque Prieto: on the GC-2 Las Palmas towards Agaete, exit 22 on the GC-295, continue on GC-294 to Roque Prieto. Las Salinas: on the GC-2 Las Palmas towards Agaete, turn onto the GC-172. The pools are on the most northeasterly part of Paseo Maritimo. | **Tip** On the southern end of Agaete promenade is the harbour Puerto de las Nieves, with its fish restaurants, beach and pier. And a famous ambience!

26 The Remote Saltworks

No white stuff makes life tough

Salt was already used as a preservative in the early Holocene, and consequently even as a means of payment. Today, a large proportion is produced for industrial use, and only a quarter ends up being consumed. The white powder is, however, essential for the human organism – essential to life. All intracellular as well as all extracellular bodily fluids contain sodium chloride. Keeping water and electrolytes in healthy balance is the premise for human life. It is not without reason that humankind is the salt in the chocolate soup and fantasy the salt in the soup of reason. Who would want to be soup when they could be salt?

The extraction of salt from seawater has a long tradition on the Canary Islands archipelago. At the end of the 19th century, salt was extracted in over 60 seawater saltworks. Today, the number has dropped dramatically: there are only around a dozen salt production plants still left. The others have been neglected, with nature doing the rest, or the sites have been used for other purposes.

Gran Canaria currently has five of these historic saltworks, which are collectively declared cultural heritage sites. 'Las Salinas del Bufadero' is the oldest on the island and the only one left on the Canary Islands that was built on rock. All the others are clay saltworks. The plot is about 10,000 square metres in size and after a renovation around the turn of the century that rebuilt the trails and mended the signage, it has once again been left to sad neglect in more recent years. The rugged surroundings are reminiscent of a martian landscape. The difference is that, apart from geological finds, you can also find artefacts here.

There are plans to get the site back into shape and to build a salt museum. The site is partly privately owned and initiatives to buy these parts back have begun. The whole thing is bound to take several years to complete.

Address Las Salinas del Bufadero, GC-2, s/n, 35413 Arucas | Getting there On the GC-2 Las Palmas towards Agaete, turn off at Vía de servicio (service exit), right before the second bridge onto an off-road area. The saltworks stretch eastwards from here. | Tip To the east of the rock tableau's gravel car park is a piece of wall from an old prickly pear finca, which is commonly known as 'Muro de la Tolerancia', i.e. the Wall of Tolerance. This section of wall stands symbolically for the building of bridges instead of walls.

27 The Crumbling Spa Hotel

Water, the noblest element, both dry and wet

This building is at least 150 years old, and it's still standing straight and true. Nonsense, that is clearly a downright lie. What is left of it today, and to be explored by the brave of heart, is a fragmented ruin. At some point in the past, sure, it was a splendid spa hotel that enjoyed an excellent reputation.

Bathing in mineral-medicinal spring water was said to have a healing effect, and people came here in droves to take the cure. Without any bravado, but certainly with fashionable bathing trunks, bi-, tan-, mono- or mankinis. The story of little Jesus, whose whole body was covered in atopic eczema, is still told to this day. Just within a week of regular bathing there wasn't a single red spot to be seen. Hallelujah!

Around the year 1900, spa hotels experienced a boom on Gran Canaria. Almost every municipality adorned itself with a wellness oasis. Visited by everyone to start with, the Balnearios mutated into purely trendy places. The well-to-do dandies, beaus and the pride of creation let the waters roll down their fur, or rather their skin, and the Champagne roll down their throats.

The building looks decidedly the worse for wear, and access to the ruin is officially prohibited. But semi-official paintball fights (for adults!) even take place here sometimes. The main gate is missing two iron bars, and a third has been bent in such a way that it is possible to slip through, if you are slender enough to be able to do so. Apart from the rubbish, fuzzy wall paintings and a murky swimming pond that is certainly no longer suitable for swimming, you will encounter, with some luck, one of the magnificent endemic butterflies that have take over and spread all around the spa hotel.

Have you ever tried ladybird soup? Maybe the older ones among you. A delicacy indeed! But butterfly soup? I'm sure that very few people know about that.

Address El Balneario de Azuaje, GC-350, s/n, 35430 Firgas | Getting there From the GC-350 between 1 and 2 kilometres onto the off-road trail at the turn by the bridge. Follow it and then continue on foot. The ruins are on the left-hand side. | Tip Barranco de Azuaje is a jungle-like maze in which you can (not) get lost. Just keep following your nose and keep your eyes open – there is so much to discover. A path leads off from the side of the Balneario in a zigzag, which will take you several metres uphill, past rock caverns and even to the town of Firgas.

28 El Faro de Punta Sardina

Experience is a lighthouse, not a lie down

Sardina, or 'sardine' in English, is not only an important saltwater fish, the product name of a snapshot camera or a restaurant in Kerobokan (Bali), but also the name of a village in the municipality of Gáldar. And in this one, on the northwesterly tip of the island, virtually at the end of the world (island), as Jules Verne might put it, is a commonplace standardised lighthouse in typical red-and-white costume.

It is neither the smallest nor the largest on the island, and it doesn't appear to be special in any other way either, apart from the fact that precisely this could be its unique selling point. It might be described among the island's lighthouses as 'el normal' – the normal one.

And yet it tells us of a fascinating contemporary conflict of interest between the state and the people. By the end of the 18th century, in exactly the same place, was a lighthouse that shone out a light to give orientation to the galleys, coastal vessels and floating wrecks of the seven seas. It was about six metres tall and part of a rectangular building, but its architecture was delightful. So beautiful and time-honoured, that an application for renovation, as well as its declaration as a cultural heritage site, was sought almost a century later.

All the ingredients for a happy ending were lined up. But no chance! Before any of this could happen, the lighthouse disappeared overnight. As if it were swallowed up by the ground or a certain, and at the time very young, David Copperfield had been at work.

What had happened? The island government didn't want to fork out a single penny for its restoration and had the building, including the lighthouse, torn down in a cloak-and-dagger operation. The only thing left of the lighthouse was a part of the floor and the memories of the experience of duelling with ruthless politicians. You probably needed to be a magician!

Address Faro de Punta Sardina, Urbanización Sau-Playa Canaria, s/n, 35469 Gáldar | **Getting there** From the GC-2 via the GC-202 towards Sardina, follow signs to Faro de Sardina | **Tip** Apart from reading Jules Verne's adventure novel *The Lighthouse at the End of the World*, this is also a wonderful place for romantic couples to catch a glimpse of the green ray (see ch. 4). South of the lighthouse is Playa Punta del Faro, a rugged pebble beach with sea pools.

29_The Infamous Necropolis

The solution is in the squaring of the circle

The Guanches were spread out over all of Gran Canaria. The island may appear small with its roughly 50-kilometre diameter and around 240 kilometres of coastline, but it's a giant compared with really small islands such as Corvo, Vadoo or Cayo Espanto. Not least due to its geographical diversity, with numerous mountains and dry valleys making it even larger than if it were as flat as a frisbee. And so it is that every few steps you take, you stumble upon a Guanches burial site.

Over the course of the last few decades, one burial site after the other has been discovered, fenced in and marked with an information board. Then that which happens so often when there are too many of something, has also ended up happening to most of the burial sites: the interest petered out. There are innumerable necropoles on Gran Canaria that no one really looks after and that are rarely, if ever, visited. They obviously still have archaeological value, and Howard Carter and Co. would surely turn in their graves if they knew, but the financial means are simply not there, nor the scientific interest and the necessary constancy and vision, to guarantee their maintenance for decades and beyond.

Gáldar – which was once called Agáldar, or 'Royal City' – is considered to have been the capital of one of the ancient kingdoms of Gran Canaria, and the citadel was home not only to a castle, but also an orphanage for girls, several strongholds and towers. However, nothing remains of this courtly complex. The philistine Conquistadores didn't care much for the preservation of pre-hispanic historical testimony. The well-known 'Cuevas Pintadas', or Painted Cave archaeological centre and this burial site on the coast survived. A locked gate is intended to obstruct access, but the fence around it has long since gone, so that you can easily enter the site off your own bat.

Address Necrópolis y Poblado de la Guancha, Calle Churruca, s/n, 35469 El Agujero, Gáldar | Getting there From GC-2 via GC-202 into Carretera del Agujero, follow the signs to El Agujero, the third exit from the second roundabout in the village, after around 100 metres the necropolis stretches out in front of you | Tip El Agujero is the name of the coastal village, but also of the complete section of the beach right next to the necropolis that has three pools and two beaches. These are to be found, unlike the Kaiser's Pool (see ch. 30), on the eastern part of the promenade.

30 The Kaiser's Pool

A stroll at low tide, a wrong turn at high tide

One is always in need of a cooling down on Gran Canaria. Benito Péres Galdós (1843–1920), one of the most famous, if not the most famous, of Gran Canaria's authors, was already well aware of this. Unless you live high up in the island's interior, and the wind blows and the snow falls like in early 2018. Yes, it's true, it does actually snow on Gran Canaria. Granted, it's not enough to ski on or even for building a snowman with a carrot nose, but the Canarios flip out nonetheless. After all, it doesn't happen every year.

Otherwise you can confidently say: get into the water and refresh yourself, with a spot of swimming or by simply letting your legs, other parts of your body or even your soul relax. And this is no different for Gran Canaria's current set of illustrious celebrities, such as Javier Bardem, Carla Suárez or Martín Chirino López. It might be unnecessary to mention this, but we are talking about bathing in the sea and not in the bathtub at home.

The pier pool, 'Piscina del Muelle', or, as the locals call it, 'Piscina del Káiser', is a sea-fed pool, that can only be identified as such by the stainless-steel ladder that leads down into it. Bathing here is, as the name suggests, imperial. At least at low tide. The surf is sometimes so wild at full tide that you may prefer to look for a spot in the sun on the pier to watch how the ladder is swallowed up by wave upon wave.

The people from the area tell the story of how football legend Franz Beckenbauer, the Kaiser himself, bathed in this pool, giving it the name it has had ever since. Let's be blunt about it: FC Bayern have twice been guests of UD Las Palmas – in the 1990s with Matthäus and in the 1970s with Beckenbauer. Bayern won the first game, and lost the second. So did the Kaiser really treat himself to a cool down in the water here after the game? It surely beats an ice bath. *¡Imperial!*

Address La Piscina del Káiser, Avenida del Agujero, s/n, 35469 El Agujero, Gáldar | Getting there From the GC-2 via the GC-202 onto Carretera del Agujero, follow the signs to El Agujero. Take the third exit off the second roundabout in the village, through the alley at the green house, 11 Calle Churruca, along the railings to the corner. The Kaiser's Pool is down in the rocks. | Tip You will find Tu Mismo, a bar like thousands of others on Gran Canaria, at the start of Calle Churruca. A little further westwards is Playa Boca Barranco.

31 Las Cuevas de las Cruces

Not seeing the cave for all the rocks

Gran Canaria and caves is like milk and muesli or yin and yang: they simply go together. But that doesn't mean, at least in the case of the caves, *que no tengan todas su encanto*, which translates roughly as 'that they don't all have their own unique charm nonetheless'. This is also the case with these caves, which aren't, strictly speaking, actually caves, but rather a long stretch of crags with crevices, cavities and cracks, a kind of Uluru with fanciful holes. Uluru? No, it's not a Swiss cheese, it's an isolated Australian mountain, also known as Ayers Rock.

The Gran Canaria Uluru isn't half as big as the original and is full of holes like a Swiss cheese, even if these days the formation of holes in cheese has noticeably declined, as there's ever less straw dust in the milk. But these rocks are absolutely fascinating. If the environmental artists Christo and Jeanne-Claude had known about these rocks, they surely would have wanted to cover them in a crazy act of art. But in contrast to other archaeological sites, the Cuevas de las Cruces have just been left behind. No signage, no information panel – in fact the hole-ly rock-cheese is barely mentioned anywhere at all.

Which is strange, because it almost seems like a work of art. In a miniature format and made of bronze it would compete with Alberto Giacometti's Chariot. There must be some record-chasing hedge fund manager or other who'd throw a million or two at something like that if it were on offer at Christie's.

As on Gran Canaria, but also elsewhere and everywhere, people just seem to simply want to throw rubbish away, and this place is certainly in need of a clean-up campaign. It's astonishing how much rubbish piles up at such fascinating places. As if the rubbish felt magically attracted by the unique charisma of this place. Undeterred by this, you can admire and enjoy the Gran Canaria Uluru. *¡Una obra de arte en piedra!*

Address Cuevas de las Cruces, GC-293, s/n, 35460 Gáldar | Getting there From the GC-2 onto the GC-293 and then it's after the first left turn on the left side. | Tip In Gáldar, at 2 Calle Audiencia, is the Museo y Parque Arqueológico Cueva Pintada, one of the most famous excavation sites on the island, which is also mentioned in relation to the 'infamous necropolis' (see ch. 29).

32__The Vibrant Vines

Wine, wine, wine, tastes so fine, purest wine

Wines don't lie, and that's why they also don't have very long noses. Whether red, white or rosé, fruity or dry, those who peddle lies and drink wine are not far from the truth. Gran Canaria's current wine-making generation are rubbing their hands, as the artistic refinement of grapes that thrive in volcanic soil is bearing fruit in the form of dazzling wines that sell like hot cakes (you wouldn't want hot wine after all).

The Bodega Bentayga, located in the Nublo Rural Park, cultivates the island's highest vineyard. Some sections of particular wine lots, barrelled in barriques of various origins, are stored in volcanic rock caves. The geographic, morphological and botanic locality of the vineyards, paired with climatic conditions that vary greatly by day and night as well as through the seasons, is a blessing for the choice grape varieties.

The Bodega Mondalón develops wines that are of equivalent quality to a French grand cru. The vineyards, where the cordon espalier-trained method based on Jules Guyot is put to use, are mainly in the historical wine-growing area of Monte Lentiscal, but also in the south of the island. The winery is one of the few on the island that has a rosé on its list.

The Bodega La Savia Ecológica operates as the island's first organic vineyard. It began producing wine in 2007 after almost a decade of labour-intensive rehabilitation of almost archaic vine varieties. Since then it has run an individual, striking series of wines, made up of a trendy trio that are so ecological and diverse, it is as if the tongue and palate take a rollercoaster ride (while already on a carousel) while listening to (or tasting) an artfully composed symphony.

Wine is grape art in a bottle, but also poisonous alcohol, so enjoy it in moderation. Or is it, seen in a sober light, only possible to bear the simulation that is life while drunk? Surely not!

Address Bodega La Savia Ecológica, 221 Calle Pío XII, 35488 Gáldar, +34 617455863, ondina@ondinasurf.com; Bodega Bentayga, Barrio Cuevas Caidas, s/n, 35369 Tejeda, +34/649941098, info@bodegasbentayga.com; Bodega Mondalón, 6 Cuesta Mondalón, 35017 Tafira, Las Palmas, +34 616655849, info@mondalon.com | Hours Tours and tastings only by previous arrangement | Tip Other addresses in other municipalities are Bodega Ansite, 26 Calle Martínez de Escobar, 35110 Santa Lucía or Bodega Frontón de Oro, Las Mesetas, s/n, 35329 La Lechuza, Vega de San Mateo.

33 The A1 Master Bakery

Where the yeast still feels the full power of the fist

'Panem et circenses', an expression uttered by Decimus Iunius Iuvenalis (or Juvenal), in modern parlance 'bread and games', is as applicable in the current day as it was back then. The distraction from social problems by the artificial dramatisation of big events, often of a sporting (and of course commercial) nature, is the order of the day. (We are the champions, etc.)

But such practices are unknown to the award-winning master bakery Amaro. Here, in well-rehearsed craft, with beads of sweat on the forehead and under the arms, according to the oldest family tradition, the dough is still pounded and kneaded by the powerful fists of a human baker. The famous-infamous 'pan de puño' is produced by means of a sophisticated fist-punch-knead-fold technique using natural raw materials. After resting and fermenting for a good one and a half hours, the lumps of dough are baked in a hot stone oven.

The stone oven that still bakes over 1,000 rolls golden brown every day is already over 250 years old. The bakery is the only one on the Canary Islands that has been named among the top 10 in Spain. Amaro and his troupe are of course particularly proud of that. But they continue to bake just as they always have. They remain straightforward and grounded – high-altitudes are for pilots.

Those who wish to indulge in this bread feast, pure or with a splash of aceite de oliva and depending on your particular diet, with jamón, queso or tofu, need to be early birds. In place of the juiciest worm, you're rewarded with the tastiest and most easily digestible bread from far and wide. But your search for a classic shop front will be in vain – the bread here is sold straight from the oven. Once you arrive in the old town of Ingenio, just follow the aromatic smell of bread through the narrow alleyways, and hey presto, you'll suddenly be standing in the bread queue.

Address Panadería Artesanal Amaro, 3 Calle el Granero, 35250 Ingenio | Getting there From the GC-100 onto Calle Los Palmeros, continue along Calle Antonio Rodriguez Medina, right onto Plazoleta del Puente, then up the steps on foot to Calle José Ramírez, first left and then right onto Calle el Granero | Tip The purest vodka in the world is produced in Ingenio. It contains 0 per cent impurities. You can't view the distillery, and you'll be pushed to find the stuff anywhere on Gran Canaria, but if a bottle of Blat Vodka should cross your path you might at least be able to astound people with your knowledge of its origins. Either way, the historic old town of Ingenio is always worth a visit.

34 The Canary Windmill

Wind, wind, whoosh, whoosh – whuu, whuu, whuuuuu

Once upon a time there was a smart inventor called Daniel Halladay, who hailed from Santa Ana in California. By night, and not by day – as his name may have suggested – he invented the iconic water-pumping windmill. And thus heralded a new era of water and power generation, all with the help of a 100-per cent natural, inexhaustible resource. And should the wind ever stop blowing, we'll be long gone, transported on the solar winds to a faraway planet. Whoosh, whoosh!

Windmills, no matter which kind, have a long history on Gran Canaria. This hydraulic Halladay-style windmill, near the airport in Las Puntillas, was made by the craftsman José Martin and is based on the Canarian model by the industrialist Manuel Santana. He is not to be confused with the former Spanish tennis player, who caused a sensation in the sport in white with the yellow felt ball in the 1960s.

The windmill is decommissioned today, but is in an excellent well-maintained condition. It stands out from the crowd due to its metallic blades, which are mounted in two rows: 45 outside and 36 inside. I counted them myself (no responsibility is accepted for the accuracy of this information). The characteristic tail fin is the dot on the 'i'. There are still a handful of wheels like this spread across the island – Halladay-style windmills were used especially on the east coast.

'When the winds of change blow, some people build walls, others build windmills' is a traditional Chinese proverb. In turbulent, irreversible times, like those we are currently unavoidably going through, one soon comes to the conclusion that there are far too many bricklayers, trampling (or is it trumpling) blindly through the world, frothing at the mouth, taking the wind out of the sails of the desperately needed allegoric windmills of the new era by being 'idiotically walled-in'. Build windmills! In great abundance!

Address El Aeromotor de Las Puntillas del Carrizal, 35259 Las Puntillas, Ingenio | **Getting there** From the GC-1 onto the GC-191, next to the roundabout parallel to the motorway feeder road, turn off into Calle Kant beforehand | **Tip** In Las Puntillas, at 17 Calle Kant, is La Casa de la Artesana, the 'Artisan Woman's House', a colourful, ornate private house (so not for visiting) with all kinds of craftwork figures and whimsical objects on the façade – a real eye-catcher from the outside.

35_The Graffiti Settlement

Taki 183, his imitators and a whole subculture

Many of us will buy a piece of art and put it in our living room, in a safe or hang it on the wall. Others wear art on their bodies. Or on house walls, as in the case of the coastal town of El Burrero. We are talking about tattoos, tattoos on walls, in other words, graffiti. The settlement is basically covered in tattoos. There isn't a street that hasn't got at least some graffiti on it. Graffiti – art or just meaningless scrawl? Or even vandalism?

Everything started, if we're talking about modern graffiti, in New York in the 1970s with a pizza delivery boy, who wrote his tag, his artist name, in other words his pseudonym, 'Taki 183', on the housing blocks he delivered to with a felt-tip pen. 'Tagging' subsequently picked up speed, also in the literal sense, and soon it was not only house walls that were tagged, but especially moving canvases: underground railway carriages. And now it wasn't only tags being scrawled, and it didn't stop with felt-tip pens. A whole graffiti movement soon developed out of the subculture of hip-hop and 'sprayed' out into the whole world.

Today, graffiti is an independent cultural form of expression, which is considered a form of art. Although this point of view does not exclude it from vandalism. Graffiti isn't in itself criminal – but the offence of damage to property is. And that is the case more often than both advocates and opponents of graffiti would like.

Many writers, as graffiti artists are called, have left behind a mark of their honour and their talent in El Burrero. Partly commissioned work, partly spontaneous, supported by some, tolerated by others and despised by others still.

A colourful mixture of tags, throw-ups and characters grace the settlement, putting their very own stamp on it. However, the scene doesn't seem to be very active any more – I hardly saw any fresh, new artworks this time around.

Address 35340 El Burrero, Ingenio | **Getting there** From the GC-1 onto the GC-192 | **Tip** In the northern part of the town, right next to a popular beach among locals, is the restaurant Terraza Club Nautico, where the gastronomical bedrocks Carlos, Gonzalo and Manolo serve up typical Canarian cuisine. Beach bar flair without the sardine-tin atmosphere!

36_The Camel Care Home

A camel rarely comes alone

Care of the elderly is seen as a barometer for the humanity of a society. In Spain, as elsewhere, there is a state of emergency in nursing, and the abuses are blatant. It isn't rare for a granny to be 'forgotten' and left on the toilet overnight, and the motto appears to be: earn good money with bad care (though I'm not implicating the carers themselves in this). But who thinks of the humble camel through all of this misery?

Where does a decommissioned camel go? No, I don't mean the dromedaries and camels that stomp through the dunes of Maspalomas in the wild, as that would be something of a Fata Morgana on Gran Canaria. I'm talking about camels who have been forced to toil and sacrifice their backs for camel safaris. In most cases the coup de grâce is employed, but a few make it here, to the camel collection pool, which is part of the 'Los Museos Vivos' project. A cultural project, initiated in 1977, that fosters the didactic-ethnographic identification and preservation of traditional Canarian culture.

The 'living museums' are spread around the whole village, and every first Saturday of the month their gates are opened to the interested public by volunteers. School classes come by on weekdays and bake bread in the stone oven, sew tablecloths or brush and feed the camels. The camels weren't foreseen at the beginning, but as there wasn't anywhere on the whole island that cared for the old camels, appropriate measures were initiated here. By the way, if you happen to be here when school classes or other groups are in action, you will be sincerely welcome to join in.

'There are camels with one hump, and there are those with two humps, but the greatest camels have none' – a quote from Arthur Schopenhauer that couldn't be more true, but the volunteers here always endeavour to care for the welfare of all camels. But they must know how to behave themselves.

Address Mejora Museo La Gañanía, Calle Cabo Verde, s/n, 35479 La Aldea de San Nicolás de Tolentino, on the corner of Calle Barranquillo de la Plaza | **Getting there** From the GC-200 onto Calle Dr Fleming towards the GC-210, first exit at the roundabout onto Calle Barranquillo de la Plata. The next road on the right is Calle Cabo Verde. | **Tip** To the northwest of the town is Playa de La Aldea with a sea pool, a park, a harbour and a handful of restaurants. It is also home to the Asociación Montymar, a source of information for divers and hikers.

37_The Canary Canyon Route

In search of lost time

Forget the legendary Route 66. And the 74, 933 and 6 too. The GC-210 on Gran Canaria, roughly 30 kilometres long, is the only real route among routes. There is no comparable route in the world. Ruth with the roots is sure to confirm what I say as long as you aren't rude. And if you still don't believe me, then ask the asphalt or Ruth's mute beaut, Knut.

That may all sound made up, but the GC-210 on Gran Canaria has got the lot. It is predominately very narrow and meanders mischievously through the mountains. It's really not for those of a nervous disposition! The rollercoaster at the Oktoberfest is, in comparison, nothing more than a caricature of the ball pools typical of Ikea or McDonalds.

At 30 kilometres it may seem short, but that's just an illusion. The route will feel much longer because you will keep wanting to stop in order to take in the view. Furthermore, the landscape changes with every blink of the eye. From agricultural plantations via bare zones to cultivated terraced fields and a pine forest, it's all there. A whole country or even a whole continent is captured along these 30 kilometres. So stop wasting your time, and get on the road.

Perhaps you think that life is too short and Proust is too long. You're right on both accounts. Marcel Proust's major work *À la Recherche du Temps Perdu (In Search of Lost Time)* can certainly be considered the Mount Everest of literature. Climbing it is fulfilling, as the Reinhold Messners and Gerlinde Kaltenbrunners of this world would surely attest, at least when talking about an actual mountain. But here you won't have any trusty sherpas at your side – you will have to read the novel all on your own. Fortunately, that doesn't apply on the GC-210, as whenever you need help, think of truthful Ruth and her cute friend Knut. Here's wishing you a good trip, with a nod and a wink!

Address The whole of the GC-210 from La Aldea de San Nicolás de Tolentino to Tejeda | **Tip** The journey isn't without its demands and can certainly be seen as an allegorical search for freedom. Immerse yourself in this feeling of freedom and let the GC-210 delight you. A stop at Mirador del Molino, after 37 kilometres, is obligatory.

38 The Stealthy Beach

Between the worlds in here and soon

Greenland has the largest (by a long way), Malaysia the smallest (followed by Germany), Tanzania the most famous (in a clinch with the USA, Canada and Australia) and Gran Canaria neither the most beautiful nor the most popular, but rather none at all. Have you guessed yet? We are talking about national parks. Unbelievable but true! Gran Canaria, unlike La Palma, La Gomera, Lanzarote and Tenerife, does not have a single national park to this day. But let's not stand for that any longer.

The Guguy Reserve (from the Berber, and translates as 'mountainous cordillera', incorrectly known as Güigüi) should have what it takes to be a national park. No question, the area is a fascinating hodgepodge in terms of flora and fauna, and the natural landscape is left to itself. But there's a catch. Nine per cent of the area, around 300 hectares, is in private hands. The owners and the island government are currently in dispute, but the latter usually has much greater leverage.

Among this reserve's real jewels are the four Guguy beaches: Playa Peñón Bermejo, which hardly a soul visits; Playa Guguy Chica, which is actually the biggest; Playa Media, on which the famous Guguy dune is to be found; and Playa Guguy Grande, where the two existing overland routes meet.

Those who allow themselves the pleasure (I have already done it seven times), to take to the path to Playa Guguy, will leave their world, whichever one it may be, behind and enter into a new, divergent one. Reality and fiction blur into a suspended feeling of freedom in ecstasy. Melancholy and resignation, happiness and vision reel a Tango bravissimo in the dance of molecules. Even better: that graceful dance, the Isa. From a step to a figure to the final chord, the heart races, the skin pulsates, and in the background a Hans Zimmer, the famous film score composer, saws the fitting notes. Lost in Guguy!

Address Playa Guguy, also Güigüi, 35478 La Aldea de San Nicolás | Getting there Two paths: the first from La Aldea de San Nicolás, the other from Tasartico, the latter is almost two hours shorter (simple route), both signposted | Tip It pays to start out good and early – certainly at some point in the course of the morning. Only by being there at low tide will you be able to walk to all the sections of the beach. What's more, you can reach the campsite and Playa Tasartico on the GC-204 past Tasartico.

39_The Winged Windmill

Windmills of your mind – hope, dream, live!

They are no longer in use, the windmills of Gran Canaria. But it isn't so long ago that these 'giants' were still performeing vital work, not just here, but on all of the Canary Islands. Mills, no matter what kind, are among the archipelago's core features. Today, most of them have disappeared, and only very few of them have been restored. They exclusively serve general museum-like educational purposes, even if one or two of them are intact, in other words, fully functioning.

The windmill in Majanos is from the year 1905 and long served as a loyal companion to the miller family. In its milling heyday, the municipality housed three hydraulic mills and ten windmills. Alongside the mill in Majanos, the mills in Machitos and Ladera are also still standing. All three can be viewed as part of the town hall's guided tours. They all stand prominently on main roads, so that viewing them from the outside is always possible.

A view of 'giants', as Don Quixote tried to convince his companion Sancho Panza in the novel *El ingenioso hidalgo Don Quixote de la Mancha (The Ingenious Gentleman Don Quixote of La Mancha)* by Miguel de Cervantes. They are only windmills, Sancho Panza protested, but Don Quixote insisted that the windmills were giants. Giants, who he could conquer by slaying them. He didn't even give up on his fantasy after the quick-spinning blades broke his lance, throwing him from his horse and sending him flying across the stone floor. Of course, for Don Quixote, it was the wizard who had transformed the giants into windmills, making it impossible for him to defeat them.

Fighting against windmills – who hasn't ever done it themselves? But hopeless battles turn out to be not even as rare as fabulous fantasies. Just as with windmills, the wind of hope always blows. And the biggest human dreams are sculpted out of hope – hope, dream, live!

Address El Molino de Viento de Los Majanos, GC-200 after 32 kilometres, 35470 La Aldea de San Nicolás de Tolentino | Tip El Charco, a wetland near the coast home to a natural pond, serves every 11 September as the location of the Fiesta del Charco. This is a festival in which hundreds of people charge into the knee-high seepage pond at the same time from all sides and try to catch a spined loach with their bare hands.

40_The British Graveyard

Hidden in the middle, not prominently uncovered

The quarter of San José isn't just any old dreary residential quarter. It is one of the oldest and most historical in the capital. Many know that, but no one is interested. But that suits the residents, because it means they can preserve their quarter in the style of their taste, don't have to put up with hordes of visitors passing through and still only observe the signs of yuppification from a distance.

In the middle of the quarter, in an inconspicuous side street, surrounded by pretty but plain houses, is the oldest piece of British history on the Canary Islands. A cute little cemetery, built in 1834 (the first burial took place in 1835), which is still meticulously taken care of to this day, and yet not visible to the uninformed. Well, those whose hairline is more than two metres from the ground may manage to get a brief glance over the wall with a spirited jump into the air.

For everyone else it's a bit of a head-scratcher, as the high wall encloses the quadratic graveyard all the way around. The British are well known for having a fine sense of humour, and this is confirmed by the many messages you can read on some of the gravestones: 'Sleeping on the island he loved', 'See you soon' and 'I told you I was sick'. The cemetery was declared a cultural heritage site in 2008.

And now here comes the magic, the Christopher Nolan trick if you will (see ch. 41), to gaining access, in two ways. The first way would be to do a MacGyver and to open the gate with the help of some pool chalk, candle wax or shoe laces, in any combination or order. The second would be to ring the doorbell of Doña Angelica at the neighbouring house to the east, hope that she is there, and to ask for the key for the cemetery gate. So, which way will you choose? I have an inkling. Doña Angelica is, by the way, getting on in years, but is always helpful. *¡Qué amable que es!*

Address Cementerio Inglés, 13 Calle Marconi, 35015 Las Palmas | Getting there L 91 towards Puerto de Mogán to Puesto Guardia Civil, then on foot northwards, left onto Calle Alicante, left onto Calle Córdoba, up the stairs to Paseo de San Jose, left onto Calle Juan Sanchez Sanchez and right onto Calle Marconi | Tip Almost right next door, to the west, is the Parque Párroco Juan Brito García. It is one of Gran Canaria's few terraced parks and the very first built in the Baroque style.

41 The Cineastic Wall

Hollywood: where broken dreams are first formed

These moments, in which where we are just extras, are not so rare. Extras in our own lives. And no director at hand for far and wide, certainly not ourselves. But then, in other moments, in which we feel we want to reach for the brightest stars, we bring ourselves back down to earth, in the best case as the director of our own dreams. Often we are grounded without a barrel, sometimes the barrel is bottomless, often it will have a false bottom. And then we must look beyond it, as a rewarding illusion is mostly hidden under a false bottom, which can also turn out to be a truth. A great master of illusion is Christopher Nolan, who always creates magic in his films.

The promise of magic is also precisely that which fills up the auditoriums annually at the start of April at the Festival Internacional de Cine Las Palmas de Gran Canaria, which has already been running for 18 years. Although saying that the auditoriums fill up isn't quite a true reflection. Like many other film festivals in the world, this one is subsidised by private and public funds. If it had to stand on its own two feet through ticket sales alone, it would sink to its knees.

This place also has a semi-permanent homage to cinema. A long yellow wall, running over two corners, allows us to be witness to 10 steps in a film production through images and additional graffiti. The work of art was created a good 10 years ago within the framework of the film festival and is a real asset of the Las Palmas street art canon. However, very few city dwellers know about it, even if they have already driven past it on a number of occasions. Often that which is hidden isn't under a false bottom, but is unfurling its blossom right in front of our eyes. Camera obscura or Laterna magica, human perception is, as we know quite well, a traitor. *¡No dejen de soñar! Sveños son dueños!*

Address El Muro Cinematográfico Hollywood, Carretera de Chile, s/n, 35010 Las Palmas | Getting there L 47 towards Tamaraceite to Carretera de Chile, right between the stop and the petrol station on the west side | Tip If you follow the Carretera de Chile further up towards Tamaraceite, take the first exit from the roundabout and then take the next two rights, you will reach Mirador del Cardón, which offers a northwest-northeast view of the city.

42_The Delightful Gan Eden

The Alma Mater of the flowering arts

Sventenius, alias Eric Ragnor Svensson, Dr David Bramwell, Bernardo Navarro Valdivielso and Dr Juli Caujapé Castells, four people who, as directors of the Botanical Gardens have given it a vision since its genesis in the early 1950s, with the idea of preserving the whole botanical wealth of Macaronesia in a large-scale garden. Mission impossible? Mission accepted! On the Canary Islands there are around 600 known botanic endemics, i.e. plants that only occur here, of which a good 90 are on Gran Canaria, and a majority of them thrive here in the Botanical Gardens. These are predominantly paleoendemic species, even if there are a few neo-endemites and even neophytes among them. The number of endemics in relation to the surface area is gigantic, and so the Canary archipelago is also described as the Galapagos Islands of flora. The garden additionally houses a variety of exotic plants, which sprout into life in cosy communality in their own garden segments. Look out for the Gran Canarian dragon tree and several varieties of the stunning blue viper's bugloss.

Two further building blocks of the garden's mission are research on one hand and education on the other. In the early days, the associated scientific laboratory was the first in Spain that had molecular biology in its repertoire. National as well as international commissions are still taken today. The Canary Islands represent an important and enlightening biotope for biologists from all around the world. A DNA bank and a germplasm bank, i.e. a seed bank, are also part of the garden's research facilities, as well as a documentation and information centre and an education centre.

A databank of endangered species is also managed, which, small wonder, continues to grow. All that counts in the end is being careful with all life on this rock we call earth. *¡Neustro planeta es hermoso y único, protéjanlo!*

Address Jardín Botánico Canario Viera y Clavijo, Calle Jardín Canario, s/n, 35017 Las Palmas | Getting there L 311 towards Santa Brigida (polideportivo) to Jardín Canario, then on foot southwestwards on Calle Piquillo, right onto Calle Jardín Canario | Hours Daily, summer 9am–7pm, winter 9am–6pm | Tip The restaurant Jardín Canario belongs to the upper part of the garden ensemble, has a terrace, offers a view over the whole site and has Canarian-Mediterranean cuisine on the menu. Flor Canaria in the lower part outside the garden is a stand-alone restaurant and offers Canarian-fusion – crafted crossover globe-trotter cuisine, so to speak.

43 The Design Façade

Creative to order, art on the bill

The world is in need of people who stop sleeping to realise their dreams. People who write history with their lives, who question that which is given, who are of the opinion that nothing is written in stone. Unfettered, passionate and brave people. People who don't just wait to be successful before they do what it is that they actually want to, but rather become big by doing precisely what they want. The world needs people who are passionate about what they do: *El mundo necesita gente que ame lo que hace*. Isleta is both the northeastern tip of Gran Canaria as well as the capital, and for a good part urbanised. The rest is predominantly a military area. Isleta already begins at the eastern section of Playa de Las Canteras, and it is precisely here that the city commissioned the creative agency 'Cúrcuma Estudio' to artistically paint an incomplete house façade with inspiring messages. The result is an ingenious design façade that is colourful and loud at first sight, but upon closer inspection exhibits many details.

It is actually quite normal to just walk past it without suspecting anything out of the ordinary – it's just a painted wall, colourful and with many motifs and lettering, but you can't stop and look at every wall that veritably begs for attention. But sometimes that attitude is simply wrong.

Another sentence that describes the Canarian philosophy of life very well, is the one next to the blue window. We Canarios love our island, and we are of the sincerest conviction that our island is paradise on earth and that there is no better place to live for far and wide, at least not on this planet. You'd be hard pressed to find a Canario who does not want to live on their island. Going on holiday or temporarily working somewhere else, yes, but living abroad permanently? No thank you! I mean, why in the world would you want to?

Address La Fachada Inspiradora Soñadora de La Isleta, 22 Calle Caleta, 35009 Las Palmas | Getting there L 1 towards Puerto to Agustín Millares Sall, then on foot westwards on Calle Peta Agustin Millares Sall, continue on Calle Rafael Benton Travieso, right onto Calle Albareda, left onto Calle Juan Rejón, continue on Calle Ferreras, right onto Calle Faro, left onto Calle Vasco de Gama, left onto Calle Concejal Manuel Rodríguez Costas, continue on Calle Caleta | Tip At 1 Calle Caleta is the highly frequented fish restaurant Amigo Camilo. And between the design façade and the restaurant are some small fisherman's huts, in which there are all sorts of curious things to see, if the artists and musicians who own them are there and grant you access or at least let you peep inside.

44_Enlightening Yoga

On searching for and finding self-awareness

The body is a temple in which the self lives. Practising yoga means revealing the self and centring body and spirit. Learning to differentiate between the self and the 'ego'. Yoga in the proper sense has little to do with what has become its common understanding: a combination of wellness and wellbeing. This merely encourages narcism and obstructs the true meaning: abstraction as a philosophical cleansing process of the self.

Alberto Jorge, owner and pioneer of Variation Power Yoga on Gran Canaria, is a Spanish yoga expert. The practices he has established propose free and creative exercises. Traditional series of exercises blend with innovative alignment, a living philosophy and ancient tradition.

In a variation of Hermann Hesse one could say that all life yearns for yoga. More exactly, it yearns for sound, harmony: resonance. Everything began with a drop of sound, the Big Bang, and the search for our self is in truth a search for this profoundly original sound by means of resonance. The *Tabula Smaragdina*, or *Emerald Tablet*, states: that which is below is like that which is above. Which means nothing other than everything flows in and back out again, but in particular that everything is possible. Forget Newton (although he did translate the text), causality is so yesterday, only possibility counts in the quantum realm. We learn the everyday world through conditioning and experiences, but it is the inner world that interprets it independently. The powerful 'ego' manifests from the self, and keeping its degeneration in check should be the most sacred of undertakings for everyone.

Alberto does specials such as Air Yoga (hanging from cloths, suspended in the air), Yoga Playa (on the beach), Hike Yoga (hiking and yoga) and Sup Yoga (on an SUP surfboard). *Cuando nada es seguro, todo es posible*, when nothing is certain, then everything is possible.

Address Power Yoga Canarias, 12 Calle Alonso Ojeda, 35009 Las Palmas, www.poweryogacanarias.com, +34 616148950 | **Getting there** L 1 towards Puerto to Agustín Millares Sall, then on foot westwards on Calle Poeta Agustin Millares Sall, continue on Calle Rafael Benton Travieso, right onto Calle Albareda, left on Calle Juan Rejón, continue on Calle Ferreras, right on Pasaje Pescadores de la Puntilla, left on Calle Prudencio Morales, continue on Calle Alonso Ojeda | **Hours** Courses Mon–Sat 9.15am–11.30pm | **Tip** Mercado del Puerto at 76 Calle Albareda is close by and is a nicely renovated covered market hall with various gourmet cuisines. But beware, for us yogis a conscious and thriving lifestyle also involves appropriate eating habits. So hands off culinary mortal sins! Feed the spirit, not your waistline.

45__The Glamorous Hotel

Five-star luxury doesn't come cheap

The beginnings of tourism on Gran Canaria go back more than 150 years. Already by the mid-19th century, culture-hungry globe-trotter fat cats came to the island of eternal springtime and savoured whisky on the rocks on its sun decks. The island was unofficially in the hands of the British, both economically and politically. It was also the British who built the first accommodation and hotels on Gran Canaria. The Hotel Santa Catalina, still run in the same luxurious tradition today, is a witness to these developments and one of the most noteworthy preserved buildings from the beginnings of the current economic motor.

After a good seven years of construction, the hotel was opened with much pomp and ceremony in 1890. It was designed by the renowned Scottish architect James MacLaren (1853–1890) in the British style of the times. But over the course of the decades the Canarian style was interwoven by the famous architect Miguel Martín-Fernández de la Torre and the artistic muralist Jesús Arencibia. So the building you see before you today is a British-Canarian hybrid, with many enchanting details on both the interior and the exterior.

The hotel has changed hands several times, most recently with legal repercussions, but the conservation of the building as a cultural heritage site is always striven for. Renovation and repair work are underway once again, all under strict preservation specifications. It is due to be reopened in July 2019.

In the meantime, however, the hotel has been almost devoured by the city. In the past, there were no other buildings within striking distance, but today it is encircled by urbanisation, apart from the park that surrounds it. If you sit on the terrace and sip on something sparkling or an aromatic distillation, blocking out the background noise of the city, there is a delightfully peaceful ambience to be enjoyed here. *¡Vivir a fondo!*

Address Hotel Santa Catalina, 227 Calle León y Castillo, 35005 Las Palmas, +34 928 243040, www.hotelsantacatalina.com | **Getting there** L 1 towards Puerto to León y Castillo, then on foot northwestwards on Calle Dr Juan Carlos Marina Fiol, feeder road to the hotel | **Tip** At the back of the hotel is the Parque Doramas, a green retreat in a well-maintained condition, with an amphitheatre that hosts open-air concerts and theatre performances throughout the year.

46__The Grand Gate to the City

Triton, tower and close contact with sand and sea

All roads lead to Las Palmas. Jean de la Fontaine and Voltaire both knew that, even if they actually said Rome. If you drive into the capital of Gran Canaria from the south on the GC-1, you will inevitably pass an unusual duo, which are connected by an alluring beach and promenade. On one side there is a 10-metre-high, 12-tonne, conch-blowing sculpture of the Greek god Triton by contemporary sculptor Manolo González. On the other, a 14-metre-long, 16-tonne, flag-bearing wind tower by the Spanish writer and composer Néstor Álamo. The whole coastal area, which used to be called Puerto de la Lasca – no, that has nothing to do with Alaska – and is now called Playa La Laja, is the grand gate to the city, even if one usually speeds past it on the motorway, completely ignoring it.

The area is, historically speaking, a real gem. This section of coast was mentioned as anchorage and beach all the way back in the 15th century. The mass of rock behind served as a quarry from the 16th century – it was stones quarried here that were used to build the city. A small settlement right on the beach and a coastal road studded with tunnels and bridges, which linked Las Palmas with Telde, were also built early on. Leonardo Torriani had already put 'La Laxa' on the map of the island at the end of the 16th century. Only at the end of the 1990s, when the motorway was extended, did it achieve its current appearance. A lot has changed and very little is reminiscent of the past.

But the older generation certainly do have memories of this place. This section of beach was the alternative to Las Canteras throughout the 20th century. My mother, for example, whose family had a small beach house here, which still exists to this day, tells me that the majority of Las Palmas locals actually preferred this beach. Fitting film title: *La La Laja!*

Address Mirador, Tritón, Torre y Playa de La Laja, 35016 Las Palmas | Getting there L 55 towards Las Palmas de G.C. (San Telmo) to Playa de la Laja, then on foot, crossing the motorway through the pedestrian underpass | Tip Right at the underpass on the coastal side there are two very new sea pools, which complement the beach and are part of the remodelling of this whole section of the coast. You can also walk the complete extended promenade to Puerto de La Luz (see ch. 52).

47_The Green Stadium

Footballers out, leisure-seeking city dwellers in

What do you do with a disused city stadium? Obvious: you turn it into a park. Well, admittedly, that wasn't the first idea, but ultimately it was the one that prevailed. In the end it took almost 12 years for work to begin. Originally the plan was to tear down the stadium completely and to build a shopping centre, which is an extremely popular development method on Gran Canaria. Believe it or not, there are currently 19 shopping centres on the island, mainly in the northwest conurbation. That's around 750 square metres of shopping centre for every 1,000 residents. Blimey O'Riley!

Gran Canaria has had a competitive first division football club since 1949, when UD Las Palmas was created through the merger of five clubs. However, UD is ultimately a yo-yo team, having already been promoted and relegated several times, including a drop down into the third tier. In the 2017/18 season, after three years in the top flight, it happened again – the club was relegated to the second division after an extremely unsuccessful season.

The fans of the club feel this pain in their hearts and souls, but all was forgotten once the first second division game of the new season kicked off. Many Canarios are football crazy, supporting their club unconditionally. The same as everywhere else in the world, where football has become more than just an agreeable leisure activity.

The park uses the whole surface of the old stadium. Parts of the grandstands were torn down in 2019, completely redesigned and incorporated into the exisiting park architecture. Lots of green with palms, flowers and trees.

A little city oasis, a small green lung, which is a welcome space for recreation, especially for the immediate neighbourhood, and is used every day both by those in search of a bit of green in their lives and by exercise junkies. A playground and a café have also been integrated.

Address Parque del Estadio Insular, Calle Pío XII, s/n, 35006 Las Palmas, surrounded between Calle Pío XII, GC-2, Paseo Chil and Calle Manuel Gonzáles Martín | Getting there L 1 towards Puerto to León y Castillo (Torre Las Palmas), then on foot northwards on Calle Leopoldo Matos, right onto Calle Manuel Gonzáles Martín to the end | Hours Daily 7am–11pm | Tip Four blocks away to the east is Playa de Las Alcaravaneras with beach volleyball courts, a magnificent view of the harbour and the neighbouring yacht harbour. The beach is Playa de Las Canteras' little sister.

48_The High-Altitude Quarter

Everything but barracked uniformed civil servants

Hoch droben auf dem Berge (High Up on the Mountain) is a dreadfully ghastly schmaltzy old film by the Hungarian actor / director Géza von Bolváry, that is very hard to stomach. Whereas up on the mountains of San Juán there is a small gem of a find, even if it isn't quite in one piece any more. The lean vestige of a quarter that was built at the start of the 20th century in the course of the Spanish–American War, a witness in best vandalised and scruffy form of an unspeakably exposed place, then as now virtually over the rooftops of the city.

What a privileged view! You can see all the way from La Isleta to Punta de Gando and from the whole channel of Barranco de Guiniguada to the mountain peaks of the island. Essentially you are standing in the middle of the city, on one of the highest central points, and you can treat your eyes to a fantastic 360-degree view. You can even make out the famous twin-towered Catedral Basílica de Santa Ana, situated right in the heart of the Vegueta quarter, which is considered the most important architectural religious monument on the Canary Islands.

A little further south are a couple of casemates from World War II, which were built during the course of the British Operation Puma / Pilgrim. After the Germans successfully took Gibraltar from the British, the British tried to seize the Canary Islands, beginning with Gran Canaria, with their own double operation. Everything turned out differently, and the military resources were deployed a little later in Madagascar, which the British took from the French in 1942. If you dare take the tightrope walk along the ridge, you will reach the Ciudad San Juán de Dios and the El Lasso settlement after a while. Continuing on the ridge you can even reach Tafira. A friend from San Juán uses the ridge as a training route. That guy really is the man!

Address El Quartel de San Juán, Calle Marfea, s/n, 35015 San Juán, Las Palmas | Getting there On the GC-5, turn right towards San Juán after the roundabout, right after the first zigzag, after more zigzags, up to the bus stop at the top; or L 54 towards San Juan to Batería de San Juan; then walk into the open land opposite the bus stop, left past the waterworks building to the barrack ruins and casemates | Tip To the south, between Calle Parróco Matias Artiles and Paseo de San José in Calle Miguel Servet, is an outdoor glass lift construction, which connects the quarters of San Juán and San José. A grotesque and unnecessary construction, which, to top it all off, is usually out of order.

49_The Idle Atlas

Sea in front, coast below, mountains behind

This guy presents himself with a bare, muscular torso, that would make the sweat pour down the forehead of many a bodybuilder. In the style of a titanic bearer of the heavens he does precisely that: he carries the sky. Where others of his kind take on pillar jobs, this specimen dedicates itself to a form of pleasant idleness. Although none of this is quite right.

El Atlante is a technically skilful sculpture by the late Canarian artist Tony Gallardo (1929–1996), which represents a woman made of volcanic rock risen from the magma, and, inspired by the myth of Atlantis, stands as a symbol for the valleys and gorges of the island. So the masterful sculpture is neither an Atlas in the classical sense nor male, and is also not a bearer of loads. The monumental, nine-metre-high rock woman heaves her chest, breathes in the heady and stimulating air of the Atlantic and stretches her arms out towards it, as if she is trying to hug the whole ocean, maybe even the whole world. There are many in the know who claim the artist worked a self-portrait into the sculpture, referring to the ponytail that he himself liked to sport.

Tony Gallardo was likewise a sportsman and a political activist, for which he spent some time in jail. He emigrated to Venezuela and lived temporarily in Madrid. But his home was and remained for all of his life Gran Canaria, and Las Palmas to be more precise and especially Playa de Las Canteras.

The experience of life on and with the beach always played a primary and positive role in Gallardo's art. This spirit was born in the early years, when he met the love of his life here. A moment for the proverbial eternity, as from then on they spent over 50 years together, going through the highs and lows of life with and for each other. Always side by side, until death decided it must tear him away from her. *Descansa en paz.*

Address El Mirador del Atlante, Carretera del Rincón, after 2 kilometres, 35010 Las Palmas | Getting there L 17 towards Auditorio to Auditorio, then on foot westwards on Carretera del Rincón, continue on the promenade for 2 kilometres | Tip The idle Atlas' direct neighbour is El Rincón del Atlante, a restaurant well frequented by local city dwellers. And in Maspalomas there is the recently reopened Parque Tony Gallardo, a large park dedicated to the artist.

50_The Immune City Beach

A reef, a lift, a piano and so much more

Pre-1883: the beach is a fundamental part of the natural and dune-covered isthmus that separates the northeast peninsula, today's 'Isleta', from the rest of the island. No buildings, far away from the city centre, barely any economic value.

1883–1960: with the beginning of the construction of the Puerto de La Luz harbour, the isthmus becomes more and more populated, the dunes disappear, the beach is christened 'Las Canteras' – in reference to the clay hollows exploited there – the whole section of beach is urbanised in phases, thus becoming the most important region in the whole archipelago. The first European bourgeois holidaymakers, mainly British and French, make their way here.

From 1960: the beach and the surrounding area is made fit for mass tourism. A good 20 years later the boom is over, and tourism shifts to the south of the island, which is successively concreted over with hotel grounds and the like. At the start of the 1990s the complete section of beach, including the promenade and adjacent roads, is reconstructed and modernised.

2000s: one of the most glamorous city beaches in the world has its finger on the pulse and serves, particularly the locals, as a blue lung and yellow heart. The natural chalk reef tongue, parallel to the beach, hosts agglomerate from the period of the transition from archaic *Homo sapiens* to modern humans, is over 100,000 years old and can be reached at low tide. A natural sea lift, 'El Ascensor', and a rock grand piano, 'El Piano', are just two of the many curiosities along the 'La Barra' reef.

I myself have spent endless hours here and done many things for the first time here: ridden my first wave, built my first sandcastle, found my first shell, had my first kiss. *¿Y cuándo fue la última vez que hizo algo por primera vez?* And when did you last do something for the first time? It's about time! *¡Por primera vez!*

Address Playa de las Canteras, 35007 Las Palmas | **Getting there** L1 towards Puerto to Tomás Miller, then on foot southwards, right onto Calle Sgto. Llagas, which leads to the promenade | **Tip** The neighbouring district of Santa Catalina to the southeast bustles with partying day and night. But there are also quiet cafés, in which you can read a book, for example the 1933 novel *Grand Canary* by Archibald Joseph Cronin.

51_The Imposing View of the City

A sight with perspective from the view with a view

Directing the view outwards while cultivating a view inwards and daring to look to the future. We should always have a vision in our repertoire, and never into dreary sluggishness. Those who live without looking, have no perspective on life. Those who this pertains to, as much as it saddens me, should be ashamed. No shrug of the shoulders is to be tolerated. Hand on heart, we owe it to ourselves. Onwards to new horizons.

Our eyes can see near and far, but it is our imagination that can move mountains. In a hole, so small and dark, in which we bury ourselves, in the here and now. We have to stand up and turn the hole into a summit to achieve foresight. Only then can we create the conditions for a better future. Our existence feeds on belief in there being a perspective. If we lose it, the darkness quickly rules over the light. What irrefutable truth.

Those who wish to savour the view here, should walk a few hundred metres up 'Montaña de Las Coloradas'. Through rugged terrain, under the spell of dry volcanic dust, in the absence of shallow idleness, onto the peak with the cross. Your soul will thank you, so colourful and distant the horizon, so powerful and invigorating the vision: the whole city at your feet. Through the circus of life, a view like 1,000 islands, Las Palmas, you are so beautiful and ugly at the same time.

The most beautiful of all prospects: so long, gone, finished and over – one may think. And yet, life is magical. The end comes to us all, so why not go kicking and screaming? And as Harry once said: 'Viele Steine, müde Beine, Aussicht keine, Heinrich Heine.' (Many stones, tired legs, no views, Heinrich Heine.) Today, more than ever, swim in the sea, all your thoughts free, perspective you'll see, can that be? Yes, if you're like me!

Address Montaña de Las Coloradas, 35009 Las Palmas | **Getting there** L 41 towards Las Coloradas to Semana de la Pasión, then on foot southwards onto Montaña de Las Coloradas | **Tip** If you follow Calle Coronel Rocha towards the sea, you'll reach Playa del Confital, the capital's secret number one beach. With a bit of luck you'll find a treasure there: the beautiful eyes of Santa Lucía alias Red Wrinklebrow *(Bolma rugosa)*.

52_Puerto de La Luz

The ocean-breeze quay

For the author of the poetry collection *Les Fleurs du Mal (The Flowers of Evil)* and pioneer of modern poetry Charles Baudelaire, a harbour is a charming place to linger for a soul exhausted in the struggle for survival. Most of us probably don't see it quite so melodramatically – a harbour is simply a place where ships arrive and depart. The truth lies, like with so many things, somewhere in between.

The origins of the harbour of Las Palmas can be dated to the end of the 15th century, the current one dates to the middle of the 19th century and work actually first began in the year 1883. It was once again the British who held the sceptre, but also the scales in their hands. They contributed the money and know-how and the Canarios provided the cheap labour. In this way one of the most important harbours in the world was created, even if it has fallen down the ranking dozens of times since then. However, the harbour is still of great importance and continues to grow. There is a logistics hub, off-shore services, shipyards, but also fishing, ferry traffic (weekly, to Cadiz on the Spanish mainland) and cruise liners, so everything a large sea harbour has in its armoury.

A harbour area has its allure, particularly if you are allowed to move more or less freely, as is the case here. It changes the perspective of the city, the country and the people. Not designed for visitors, but also not closed off. You can walk around most of the quays, and drive into some. The outermost is named after Nelson Mandela, the longest after Queen Sofía of Schleswig-Holstein-Sonderburg-Glücksburg.

I can still remember very well how I walked through the harbour as a child, usually with my siblings, holding papa's hand. Dawdling through the harbour was a tradition and it was always great fun. A tradition that the new generation also experiences. *¡El Capitán Trueno!*

Address Puerto de La Luz, 35008 Las Palmas | **Getting there** L 1 towards Puerto to Manuel Becerra, then on foot eastwards, right onto Calle Dr. Antonio Jorge Aguiar, third exit at Plaza Belén María onto Avenida Juan Rodríguez Dorestes, first exit at the roundabout onto Explanada Tomás Quevedo, second exit at the roundabout (Muelle de Leon y Castillo) | **Tip** There is harbour small talk par excellence in the El Muelle restaurant. And the Armas ferries depart from Muelle Nelson Mandela, sailing to the other Canary Islands several times a day as well as the Spanish mainland and soon Madeira too.

53 The Running Festivals

Burn up the trail path till your shoes smoulder

Walking, running, jogging and recently trailing, or trail running. First recognised by the IAAF as an official discipline in 2015, people have of course been running up hill and down dale since time immemorial. It used to simply be called hill running. But today it is trail running and it has experienced an unbelievable hype in recent years.

One of the most important international trail running meets is now the Transgrancanaria, a trail competition that was initiated back in 2003. Now, more than 15 years later, it is a fixed date on the elite trail calendar, but thanks to races over shorter distances and less demanding routes, the competition also enjoys huge popularity among amateurs and beginners. Gran Canaria, with its unique landscape, offers ideal conditions for such competitions. The sport has long since delighted the masses, and the Canarios are completely dedicated to recreational trail running, making use of the whole island in the process.

Hiking has been able to generate at least as much popularity. Those who think anything of themselves spend the weekend climbing a mountain or taking on a walking tour through forest and meadow. Gran Canaria is the ultimate hiking paradise, and little by little a number of hiking routes have been established, including the Walking Festival, which was launched in 2012. Various hiking tours, leading through the island's most wonderful areas, are on offer over several days.

Sure, Gran Canaria means lots of beach, sun and sea, and that's a good thing, but it isn't without reason that the Canary Islands have been spoken of as a miniature continent for decades. That is very much the case on Gran Canaria, and you can only understand what is meant by that if you too widen your horizons off the beaten track. Beach loungers versus trail walkers! Get your backsides in gear!

¡Quien no se mueve muere! ¡Vamos!

Address Festival offices: Transgrancanaria, Calle Urbanización Industrial Díaz Casanova, s/n, 35010 Las Palmas, www.transgrancanaria.net; Gran Canaria Walking Festival, Calle Los Balcones 4, 35001 Las Palmas, www.grancanariawalkingfestival.com | Tip The ocean trail has several paths along the water's edge and on the rocks of Playa El Confital, including its jetty promenade. I run it regularly in the morning when the sun slides slowly over the Isleta hill into the sky and kisses the city awake. Am I the man too (see ch. 48)? By no means!

54_The Solitary Watch Tower

Once upon a time there was a sperm whale…

…that beached slap bang in front of the San Cristóbal quarter in the middle of the 1960s. The story did the rounds of the whole island, as it took a few days before it was able to free itself and return to the depths of Neptune's kingdom. The only thing that it left behind, apart from the sensation that stuck in people's heads, was the nickname that was given to residents of the quarter from then on: the sperm whales. Yes, wasn't that creative?!

Today, the quarter is the only one in the capital that defines itself predominantly by fishing, although these days it is more its fish restaurants that it's is known for right across the island. The name of the quarter comes from the times of the conqueror Cristóbal García del Castillo and his freebooters and pirates. The proud legacy of the belligerent conquistadores, a fortified castle, is also from the 16th century. Although at this point the truth must be told: the only part of the castle that remains is the watch tower of San Pedro Mártir.

Nonetheless, it is a powerful piece of history that has defied the ravages of the sea for centuries. It is located on the outermost edge of a rock tongue and protrudes several metres into the sea. A really powerful fortress that proved impenetrable at the time to Francis Drake, a 'pirate' hated by the Spanish. On the orders of Elizabeth I, he was to conquer the castle, but he failed in all his attempts.

There aren't any pirates these days, and the solitary watch tower has been declared a cultural heritage site and now marks out its existence in the shadow of hungry mouths. The quarter is made up of around 60 houses, and the number of residents is about three to four times that, but when it comes to the weekend, the car park spaces tend to fill up. This is when the hungry city dwellers come and eat the kitchens of the nine fish restaurants empty. *¡Pescado para todos!*

Address Torreón de San Pedro Mártir, 35016 San Cristóbal, Las Palmas | **Getting there** L 12 towards Las Palmas de G.C. to San Cristobal, through one of the alleys eastwards to Promenade Calle Marina, then follow it left to the end | **Tip** Fish, fish or fish in thousands of variations – that's what all the cooks have in their pots or pans. No matter which restaurant you happen to stumble into, there's something for every fishy palate. Some are rustic, others more classy and others again more family friendly or etiquette loving. Simply follow your fish nose. And at the southern end of the quarter is the muelle, the small pier.

55_The Sports Lovers' Park

Body cult and cult bodies

Las Palmas is a sports-crazy city. The people here have an irrepressible urge to move and pursue their sport both on land and on the water, but especially outside in the open air. There are dozens of sports clubs and an abundance of open spaces and parks.

An extremely popular sports meeting place is 'Parque Romano', which serves hundreds, if not even – and I'm leaning out of the window a little here – thousands of sporty people as the place to sweat it all out every day. A two-lane, 500-metre-long stretch of earth-sand is divided by a green palm middle bed and flanked by a grassy tree and shrub alley. There is fitness equipment positioned on the side lawns, and a street work-out zone is there for people to carry on fitness training methods such as CrossFit, calisthenics or that exercise programme of the moment, BodyBoss.

The park serves as a training location for many sports groups, which leads to a multicultural sports scene and creates a fruitful atmosphere of solidarity. All manner of people arrive throughout the day, from personal trainers with their charges to running groups, school classes or sport cliques armed with loudspeakers. Whether it's cold or warm, come rain or shine, there are always people training here.

And of course you mustn't forget the corresponding post on the internet. Selfie here, selfie there, post it out into the matrix, because doing something without others being aware of it, well, those days are long gone. What one does shouldn't simply fizzle out in the face of not documenting it – after all, in many cases, you would then never do it again and thus choke on inactivity.

The Parque Romano was completely redesigned in the first half of 2019 and now appears in all its modern splendor, without losing the ambience of an outdoor workout space. No pain, no gain! Shut up and train! Aim high!

Address Parque Romano, Terracera Leon y Castillo 270, 35005 Las Palmas | Getting there L 12 towards Hoya de La Plata to Alc. J. Ramírez Bethencourt (Parque Romano) | Tip To the south of the sports lovers' park is Club Natación Metropole, which houses the island's first swimming pool within its large complex, which used to belong to the former Hotel Metropole. The club does not run a leisure pool, but non-members can also take part in certain courses or crawl through the water in the limited free-swim periods.

56_The Striking Allotment

Beware! Poison dwarves instead of garden gnomes!

Have you ever heard of urban gardening? Of course you have! Everybody is talking about it and it has been a central aspect for greener and more sustainable consumption for years among the do-gooders of the modern era. And of course this concept also plays a role in a modern, vibrant capital like Las Palmas. In fact, several spots have arisen in recent years and now blossom in the shadow of concrete residential blocks.

This urban garden is a flagship of its kind, as the hobby gardeners, who managed to get hold of a plot really care for them, and produce a bountiful harvest. But it also serves as a role model in other respects, because when the question of how to use the wasteland in the middle of the city arose, the investment-crazy developers were queueing up to realise a luxurious residential building, with 187 storeys if they could get away with it! But the residents fought back and after a lengthy dispute, in which the fat cats were defeated in something of a huff, the building of the striking allotment was initiated.

But the aim was to put the plot of land to a wide range of uses, not only for gardening. And so a small park including a children's playground was integrated. The residents are delighted and love their little bit of green between all the house fronts.

Urban gardening is, however, in no way new or a pastime reserved to hip vegans. After all, this kind of gardening has been carried out since the first cities were built. Allotment culture is a good example, mostly pushed out to the periphery of cities these days, but there are also all kinds of allotment colonies in inner-city areas. Even in metropolises such as New York, London and Berlin. But what doesn't seem to have caught on in Gran Canaria is the garden gnome! There are, however, thieving poison dwarves, who help themselves to produce straight from the vegetable plots. What pests!

Address Huerto Urbano Parque Pino Apolinario, 15 Calle Portugal, 35010 Las Palmas | **Getting there** L 1 towards Puerto to Eduardo Benot, then on foot to the south towards Calle Alfredo L. Jones, right onto Calle Luis Morote, left onto Calle Nicolás Estévanez, left onto Calle Fernando Guanarteme, right onto Calle los Martínez, left onto Calle Portugal | **Tip** Paseo Las Canteras, the Playa de Las Canteras promenade, runs parallel to Calle Portugal. It offers a moving ambience at any time of day and the promise of delightful idleness. The locals usually hold the upper hand here; they love their city beach promenade, even in the evenings, for hours of dancing, hanging out and fun.

57_The Vibrant Museums

Museuming through Las Palmas

Some complain about greying dusty museums, others prefer to watch Hollywood slapsticks about nights in museums at the cinema, and others still want to have their eyes opened and horizons widened. They let themselves be taken in by the arrow of time and space-time, to feel the essence of time, to strengthen their awareness of self, immerse themselves in the art of leisure.

A visit to a museum does not have to be that slice of dry bread lost behind an abandoned Billy bookcase. Museums, especially today more than ever before, emanate the true spirit of the Zeitgeist: or don't the majority of us exhibit ourselves constantly these days. Aren't we virtually our own museums? 'Give me a museum and I'll fill it,' Picasso once said. And in this sense, it is the custodians and curators who fill the museums today. And everyone else fills the internet.

Believe it or not there are over 70 museums on Gran Canaria. There are no fewer than 15 in Las Palmas alone. The only municipality currently without a museum is Mogán. The historical and ethnographic Museo Canario with its dinky little museum shop, housed in a stylish old town palace, is the capital's museum flagship. It is located in the heart of the old town quarter of Vegueta, not far from the cathedral.

From the airport, straight to the museum to take in an audio-tour – this is the only way you can understand immediately which patch of the earth you've landed on. Of course no one does that, but that doesn't make it any less true. The figure *El Ídolo de Tara*, installed in the museum, is world famous.

Further notable and vibrant museums are the Fundación Martín Chirino, located in Castillo de La Luz, the CAAM and the Casa-Museo Pérez Galdós.

'Build not an empire where everything is perfect! "Good taste" is a virtue of the keepers of museums,' as Antoine de Saint Exupéry once said. Museum tastefully!

Address El Museo Canario, 2 Calle Doctor Verneau, 35001 Las Palmas; Castillo de La Luz, 37 Calle Juan Rejón, 35008 Las Palmas | Getting there L 12 towards Hoya de La Plata to Mercado de Vegueta, then on foot to the southeast, right onto Calle Roque Morera, left onto Calle Espíritu Santo, left onto Calle Reloj, left onto Calle Dr Verneau; L 12 towards Puerto to Augustín Millares Sal, then on foot eastwards, left onto Calle Mahón, left onto Calle Juan Rejón | Hours El Museo Canario: Mon–Fri 10am–8pm, Sat, Sun & holidays 10am–2pm; Castillo de La Luz: Tue–Sat 10am–7pm, Sun & holidays 10am–2pm | Tip Near Museo Canario, on Plaza de Santa Ana, is the famous Catedral de Santa Ana. Put this book down for a moment and simply let yourself be affected and swept along by the flair of this magical, museum city.

58 The Bustling Sea Grotto

For bathing clowns, mermaids and champion swimmers

This place is a real bull's eye for water lovers. Tauro, 'bull' in English, is the name of the village, the beach and also the sea grotto, all of which are to be found near the sunshine location of Puerto Rico. To the left of the beach along the coast is a natural sea grotto, the like of which you'll otherwise only ever see in National Geographic documentaries about the miracles of nature. Entry requires a bit of courage, but there are stalactites, shells and fossils as a reward. And maybe a few crabs, starfish and snails too. Bon appétit!

A visit to the grotto is to be recommended at low tide. After all, it is pretty much full of water at high tide. The openings are so large that you can even paddle through them in a canoe. The grotto is extremely popular among locals, especially the younger generation, as is the rock formation immediately in front of the opening, which they use as a stage for cliff jumping. At low tide the water appears not to be deep enough, but your eyes deceive you. Ultimately you will be able to judge what's what by watching the experienced grotto visitors.

There are countless sea cavities of various sizes along the entire coast of the island. It is particularly the divers and snorkellers who keep discovering new underwater caves and sea grottoes. News of most of them, just like this one, spreads quickly. But hardly any of them have been declared cultural heritage sites by the island government, which is exactly the opposite of what happens with the cave finds on land.

Nonetheless, these finds, formed by the sea, are highly rewarding places that show us yet another side of the island and one that sometimes does not get the greatest attention: Poseidon's kingdom! Gran Canaria's underwater world is just as exciting as that of Zeus. The coast is home to unparalleled natural riches, and a look under water is always worthwhile.

Address La Cueva Bufadero de Tauro, Lugar Playa de Tauro, s/n, 35138 Mogán | **Getting there** GC-500 Carretera Mogán, after 75 kilometres follow the Playa de Tauro path to the beach. On the southern section on the rocky shore underneath the first elevation. | **Tip** There is a bar right by the beach, where things start to get interesting in the second half of the day. PS: Take your snorkelling equipment with you. And an underwater iPhone if you've got one. What? You haven't got an Instagram account? Then Twitter. Not on there either? That only leaves the data leech Facebook! You can't fob me off with a measly Whatsapp message!

59 The Laconic Beaches

Playa Guguy's little sisters

Those who find the way to Playa Guguy (see ch. 38) too long, or the walk that is necessary to take disagreeable, can content themselves with its little sisters, Playa de Tiritaña and Playa Montaña Arena. The amount of walking to both is infinitely less and can be achieved without great effort. The former is about a quarter of an hour over open terrain, over stone and rock, and then through a narrow gorge. So Kneipp sandals, high-heeled cork sandals or plastic flip-flops are not advisable, but I've seen them all. The way to the latter is along a clifftop path and is about half as long.

Both are prime examples of unspoiled beaches that remain largely undiscovered. Even if some of you, and in particular the internet, will now make fun of me for that. What remains 'undiscovered' for more than five minutes these days? However, both beaches are by no means overcrowded.

A good friend of mine spent countless weekends or even weeks of the holidays as a child with his family in the 1970s and 1980s on Playa Montaña Arena, armed with a tent, gas cooker and everything you need in a place that has neither power nor running drinking water. At that time the 'eponymous' wall of sand behind you was at least twice as big, and at full tide it could get a little tight. Then it was a natural beach hideaway for locals, and today it's for anyone who likes sleeping under the stars. Wild camping allowed? More like tolerated!

Playa de Tiritaña is located in a dreamy picturesque bay, the water is crystal clear, there are stones and rocks lying around everywhere, also on the first metres towards the open sea, and it is surrounded by cliffs. A bit rugged at high tide, so bathing at low tide is preferable. There are of course neither restaurants and bars nor any other facilities here.

This doesn't make the beaches more unpopular, but certainly more untouched.

Address Playa de Tiritaña, GC-500, between 40 and 41 kilometres, 35138 Mogán, path leads off the road at the bend; Playa Montaña Arena, GC-500, gravel car park after 23 kilometres, continue on foot to the sea, clifftop path along the coast to the left | Tip For those who can't get enough of the more than 100 beaches on Gran Canaria: Playa de Medio Almud. Also on the GC-500, basically Tiritaña's neighbour. Between 39 and 40 kilometres, an asphalted road turns off at the bend, but a barrier blocks the entrance, so here too the last stretch is on foot.

60_The Secret Treehouse

High up in the trees swings a sprite

It was many years ago. To be honest I was still a kid. As so often happened, the weekend was not spent at home in front of the telly or the games console, with Lego bricks or with the combing and brushing of Barbie, Ken and co., but rather outside on the beach, on a country estate or, like this time, high up in the mountains. In 'Los Tilos de Moya', a nature reserve, to be more precise, in which one of the last remnants of the 'Laurisilva', the Canary laurel forest, which belonged to the 'Selva de Doramas', the Doramas jungle, more than 500 years ago, is to be found.

I'm a laurel tree, get me out of here! No, no, it wouldn't have happened quite like that. But the jungle did actually disappear little by little, thanks to humankind and its interventions in nature. In the 1980s the destruction was so advanced that the island's government declared today's 'Los Tilos de Moya' a prohibited zone and carried out reforestation. Today, the protected area is once again a unique forest sanctuary.

We started our walk that weekend at the 'Centro de Interpretación de Los Tilos de Moya', from where many hiking paths lead off. And what did we discover at some point somewhere in the middle of nowhere? A spectacular treehouse! It was very high up in the trees, and a liana vine hung down from it. The squirt Rolando, begging his mum and dad to let him climb up, got the okay. And what jumped down towards me? A forest sprite! What a shock! And Rolando flew down and plopped into the arms of his quick-reacting dad.

I have now tried several times to find the treehouse, but sadly without any success. But it is there, there's no doubt about that. I think I was very close to it, as the picture on the right clearly shows treehouse equipment. Try your luck! And if you find the treehouse, I'll get a tattoo of it, or I'll invite you for an ice lolly.

Address Los Tilos de Moya, Centro de Interpretación de Los Tilos de Moya, 15 Camino los Tilos, GC-704, 35421 Moya | **Getting there** From the GC-700 onto the GC-704, after 100 metres on the right side | **Tip** By the way, Los Tilos de Moya is worth every second, even without finding a treehouse. Right on the crossroads of the GC-700 and the GC-704 is the restaurant Los Tilos, where the Canarian rabbit is one of the real hits. PS: I don't want to be so stingy, so instead of an ice lolly I'll treat you to a lavish dinner at my place. *¡Quien busca encuentra!*

61 The Uber-Popular Restaurant

Here, above the clouds means above the sea

It is so well known that it should probably have come back full circle to obscurity again. Having said that, with such a prominent location it can hardly hide itself, and the human craving for spectacular places is also seemingly insatiable. In fact, this restaurant is known primarily because of its location on the outermost point of the El Roque settlement, which was pretty much built on a rock spur.

But a location can be as idiosyncratic as it likes; what really matters to a restaurant in the end is the food and the service. What can I say – just like everywhere else, they only cook with water here, but nevertheless they still walk away with full marks. Here good food and good service are coupled with an extravagant ambience.

Sometimes people accept the good half-hour drive from the capital in order to enjoy a great meal here in good company. As if there weren't enough gastronomical treats in Las Palmas! But coming here has a certain charm and opens the way to a sea-breeze atmosphere that you won't find anywhere else. It is a small tidy restaurant, unpretentious, rather casual and laid back and yet with style and certainly a touch of class.

The restaurant has been run for a good 10 years by an Italian globetrotter and his family. No, not your typical mama Italia family, but rather a free-spirited patchwork family. The menu is small, the food selective, with lots of fresh produce, fish and other seafood, and the espresso comes from a percolator, better known as the moka pot.

You may laugh, but as luck would have it, I had never come across this uber-popular restaurant before. Unbelievable but true. So I went straight over there, discovered the restaurant's charm and met its charming owners. There will soon be a change in management, but that surely won't stop this restaurant from delivering the goods. *¡Hasta pronto!*

Address Locanda El Roque, 58 Calle El Roque, 35413 El Roque, Moya, +34 928 610044 | **Getting there** GC-2 Las Palmas towards Agaete, exit 15, sharp right at the roundabout onto the car park. On foot through the narrow alleyways to the northernmost point. | **Hours** Tue–Sat 10.30am–midnight, Sun 10.30am–7pm | **Tip** A few hundred metres to the west of El Roque is the coastal area of San Lorenzo, which includes a sea swimming pool and a surfing school.

62__The Brazen Mill Aqueduct

Waterless mill will leave you speechless

'Cada cual encamina el agua a su propio molino', according to a Spanish idiom, which means everyone directs the water to their own mill. That's the way it was here too, back in the 19th century, including in the winding form of an ingenious aqueduct. Built with girders of stone and pinewood, the water flowed along the aqueduct and fell a good 12 metres onto the blades, powering the mill mechanism. Very clever, but an old trick nevertheless.

As we already know, windmills and wheels (see ch. 34 and 39) have a long history on Gran Canaria, and the same can be said for watermills. These were run mainly as flour mills, at least until the motor took over and the archaic work gave way to technological advances. Today there isn't a single miller family on the island that still uses the power of water in the production of gofio (Canarian flour – be sure to try it!). We are writing in the year 2019 after all, and look futuristically towards fully automated milling systems.

And to other exciting inventions promised by the future, like, for example, space tourism or the self-flying air taxi. Or how about a virtual journey? We'd still rather be there ourselves, right? It's a bit like this book – holding it in your hands is different from reading it on a black screen or uploading it directly to your brain.

But the future will catch up with us all, whether we want it to or not. At the very latest, our children's children will shake their heads and laugh about us and our antiquated existence. But I'm sure I could interest you in a trip into space and back. Then all you have to do is to get a copy of the soon to be published guide *111 Places in Space That You Must Not Miss*. Here's a small preview of some of those places: Olympus Mons, the Carina Nebula as well as the black hole at the center of the Milky Way.

Address Monumento El Molino de Agua de Cazorla, GC-60, s/n, 35108 Fataga, San Bartolomé de Tirajana | Getting there On the GC-60 between 30 and 31 kilometres | Tip El Molino de Agua finca is an ecologically-run holiday residence in the middle of the Fataga valley basin, from which the watermill got its name, and is located only a stone's throw from the brazen mill aqueduct. A footpath connects both.

63 The Cosmic Relics

The solar system so near yet so far

José García, member of the Meteoritical Society and passionate meteorite hunter, owns the third-largest collection of meteorites in Spain. Pieces that came from far away out in space and are witnesses to our origin: the cosmos. That alone is impressive. But this guy doesn't simply just keep these cosmic things under lock and key; instead he opened a private meteorite museum without further ado.

José had his rooms in Arinaga for a good three years, but has had to close. He is now looking for new premises for his cosmic messengers in the south of the island, and hopes to make the move by 2019. So keep your eyes open – his collection is first class and absolutely unique on the Canary Islands.

The collection doesn't only contain meteorites, but also tektites, impactites, moldavites and thin sections and other cosmic storytellers that have fallen from the sky. Speaking stones that tell us lots about the creation of the cosmos and the planets. The prehistoric rocks of our solar system tell complicated stories that bring us a step closer to the truth. These time capsules are mostly 4.5 million years old, corresponding to the age of the solar system. Around 20,000 of them pelt the earth every year, but mostly go undetected, splashing down into the sea for example. Only around five a year are sighted and documented. They are extremely hard to find and very valuable. Most recently they have even been traded as investments.

You can find all sorts in such a meteorite. Traces of Mars' atmosphere sealed in black glass or magnetically structured crystals. But not all meteorites are made equal. The most common form is the stone meteorite, followed by the iron meteorite, and then the very rare stone-iron meteorite. José García knows them all, hunts them all over the world and presents them in sporadic exhibitions. And what do you hunt? Surely not ducks (see ch. 65)?

Address Museo Canario de Meteoritos, lost in San Bartolomé de Tirajana, new location currently not found, so put it on your list and keep your eyes peeled | Tip José García and his boys launched the paper *Meteoritos* in 2017. Via the website www.meteoritoscanarias.blogspot.com you can subscribe to have the paper, which is published at irregular intervals, sent to you free as a file or read it directly online. Otherwise give in to something completely different: the Yumbo Centrum, the legendarily tacky shopping centre.

64_The Cosmos Seer

The orbit's always in view

Here is a space centre that you can't touch. El Centro Espacial de Canarias is actually impossible to miss, and yet pretty much no one knows what exactly this complex, weighed down with antennas and telescopes, is. Something to do with the universe, but that is usually as much as you will get.

It is a private area that is closed off by high fences and billions (at least!) of cameras. So just popping by and ringing the bell isn't really possible. A clearly visible sign prohibits mere mortals from far off from following the road. But you can certainly get a good look at it from some places around it, and you can approach the site easily, without having to fear you'll be bumped off or that you'll find yourself in front of a top-secret NASA facility like the one in Christopher Nolan's space exploration epic *Interstellar*.

Although NASA is the right keyword here, as it was NASA itself that negotiated a deal with the Canarios in the 1950s as part of the first manned space programme in the world – Mercury – and who built the space centre at the start of the 1960s. In 1975, NASA said adiós or probably just goodbye, and the site was left to its own devices for the time being. It was four years before the Instituto Nacional de Técnica Aeroespacial opened a branch office here. Today, the space centre is a recognised facility in the global network of the three most important space agencies in the world: NASA, ESA and JAXA.

The centre does in fact receive visitors, school classes or student delegations, but sadly the gates stay closed to the classic wanderer. Innumerable satellites are controlled from the space centre, but its duties are manifold. Capturing radio signals, receiving images of the earth, measuring sea temperatures and much more. A secluded place in turbulent Maspalomas that hardly a soul cares about, but where space is always being observed.

Address Centro Espacial de Canarias des Instituto Nacional de Técnica Aeroespacial (INTA), Calle Los Pasitos, s/n, 35018 Lo Blanco, San Bartolomé de Tirajana | **Getting there** GC-500 between 20 and 21 kilometres, right at the roundabout towards La Montaña Blanca, follow the road right to the top, on a hill behind Bar Aridañy | **Tip** On the coast, south of the space centre, is Playa de Las Mujeres. Extremely popular among locals and despite the name 'the women's beach', men are also welcome. As are all other gender types. Evolution is diversity!

65 The Duck Pond

All kinds of ducks, except Peking

No, Maspalomas doesn't only have beaches, sea and sun and disagreeably ugly residential areas on offer. I mean, it does have all of those, but there are also agreeably pretty domiciles, as well as contrasting points on its programme, for example Parque Urbano del Sur with its duck pond. If you've had your fill of sand between your toes, why not go on a duck hunt?

Although when I say hunt, I don't mean you should try shooting down your dinner here. It's enough if you look out for the ducks, photograph them or simply just watch them. Isn't that exactly what people do all over the world? Who has never fed dabbling ducks before? I expect the number with hands aloft to be around the zero mark.

These ducks have even had the pleasure of greeting some international celebrities, for example the Norwegian Trond Nymark. Trond who? Okay, I admit that only the dyed-in-the-wool fans of 50-kilometre walking will know this exceptional athlete, who, rather untypically for walkers, does not shave his body hair, yet does have a bald head. Like him, there are many jogging enthusiasts who use the 6,500-square-metre park as a running track. Yes, I too have run here once, but considering my level of fame, the ducks clearly didn't give a quack. The park, which covers an area of less than a hectare, also has a climbing rock, a terraced restaurant and a playground.

According to unverified sources, there are descendants of Donald Duck living among these ducks. Apparently, a part of his family emigrated to Gran Canaria in the 1950s. There is no proof. However, a group of duck enthusiastic ornithologists have banded together in an attempt to get to the bottom of the tail (er, tale). Quack, quack, quackers! But even without Donald's ducks there are various species to marvel at here. With a bit of luck you might even spot a black-necked grebe. *¡Qué guay! ¡Eso sí que mola!*

Address El Lago de Los Patos, Parque Urbano del Sur, Avenida de la Unión Europea, s/n, 35100 Maspalomas, San Bartolomé de Tirajana | Getting there Between the quarters of San Fernando and Sonnenland, entrances on the GC-500, the GC-503 and Avenida Alejandro del Castillo. The duck pond is in the southwest of the park. | Hours Daily 10am–11pm | Tip Music and other kinds of events regularly take place in the park. Those who can't get enough of parks should visit the botanical gardens around the corner at 2 Avenida Touroperador Neckermann too.

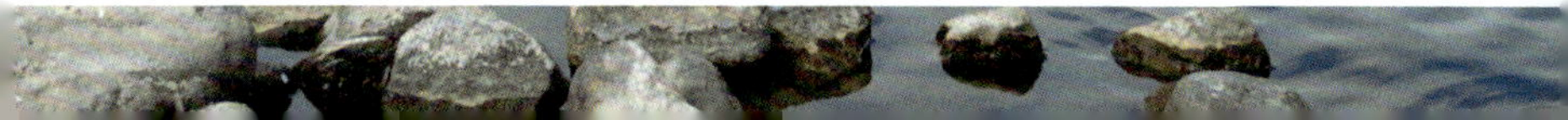

66_The Muddled Waiting Room of Souls

Masterful genre syncretism in breathless flair

There are waiting rooms for souls in almost every culture. Since far back to the beginnings of human communities, being laid in the ground at your death has been a widespread phenomenon, although columbaria are also popular. There is certainly no shortage of burial sites anywhere – people are always dying after all. Sure, the way it is done can be very varied, 'how' is the mother of all possibilities, but whether this way or that, this thing called life comes to an end for all of us at some point. Death, he comes for us all and properly grounds us, levelling us all. It is more than just an end product of ageing, an important part of our lives and culture; it embodies the inevitable result of every human life.

This graveyard, built in a neo-Gothic eclectic style on Monte Pibre – El Cementerio de Tunte – was already declared a cultural heritage site in 1996, and its construction dates back to the end of the 19th century. A rectangular piece of land a good 3,000 square metres in size with two parallel plots, with a mortuary, burial ground and chapel are marked off by a rammed earth wall. The ornamental details of the façade are inspired by the Middle Ages and also feature medallions, borders, ornamental elements and Celtic crosses, which can be categorised as Gothic and due to the blend of architectural styles, eclecticism.

Here we have a 'muddled waiting room of souls', which makes a recreational visit, as opposed to a dead visit, into an architectural journey into historicism. The very last journey, on the other hand, still remains a mystery for us who remain on this side. The essence of death is cloaked in deep mystery. We enter into the world as mortals and will catch a cold along the way, but also ultimately death. At the end, life and existence are no more than a disruption to non-existence. *¡Que viva la vida!*

Address Cementerio de Tunte, Calle San Juan, s/n, 35290 San Bartolomé de Tirajana | Getting there From the GC-60 onto the GC-603, continue on Calle el Roque, then left onto Calle San Juan, entrance on the left side at the crossroads to Calle Escaleritas | Hours Daily 8am–5pm | Tip Left of the main entrance, at the end of the wall, a footpath leads off to a hill, from where the view is breathtaking.

67_The Tears of St Lawrence

Look, stare, gape and goggle

And we continue with the spaced-out extraterrestrial theme – after all, all good things come in threes. After the meteorite museum and the space centre (see ch. 63 and 64) it is now the turn of some cosmic tears.

We are the only living beings that can cry due to emotion. Joy, pain or sadness: a human being sheds an average of 100 litres of tears during their lifetime. But be careful, as 'shed' has negative or at least wasteful connotations, so let's say 'produce' instead. That's because tears cleanse the soul, regulate the psyche, create empathy among others and filter, clarify and iron out our feelings. Crying is one of our basic forms of expression, and all the tears that we don't let roll down our cheeks drown our heart in the long run. So then, have you cried yet today, or should we say produced any tears?

The tears of Saint Lawrence, who died a martyr's death on 10 August, 258, have managed to gain celebrity. This Roman deacon gave his name to the annual cosmic fireworks that are generally known as the Perseids. This meteor shower (once believed to be the saint's burning tears) that is made up of a stream of debris from the comet 109P / Swift-Tuttle, orbits the sun as a cloud of particles and is crossed by the earth every year between July and August.

The graceful Cassandra of antique mythology, equipped with the gift of prophecy, interpreted the 'fire in the sky' as the sign of a bloody future.

We have been much wiser on the matter since the Middle Ages: shooting stars are lucky charms. But not everywhere: Mongolians, for example, still see them as messengers of misfortune. Nevertheless, make a wish – you can always count on the Perseids. It will be several thousand years until Swift-Tuttle completely disintegrates. Mirador de la Degollada is an easily-reached place to send your wishes out into the universe. *¡Llorar!*

Address Mirador de La Degollada de La Yegua, GC-60, s/n, 35107 San Bartolomé de Tirajana | **Getting there** GC-60 after 7 kilometres | **Tip** Gran Canaria offers fantastic conditions all year round for watching the night sky (see ch. 110), especially in the southern part, as the sky is mostly clear. Further south on the GC-60 is the open-air museum Mundo Aborigen, which feels like it's been there for hundreds of years. It is one of the island's early touristic theme parks, a reconstruction of a Guanches village.

68_The Vanishing Dunes

Capturing yourself in the charm of a pile of sand

There you are, standing in the middle of the dunes, feeling the tingle of sand between your toes and what do you do? Exactly, take a selfie! Or lots of selfies. You can rarely be satisfied with the first one. A dune selfie? Splendid! The dunes of Maspalomas are among the island's most famous natural landmarks, and nothing quite compares: you just have to stand on a pile of sand like this yourself.

How many times have I stood on these dunes? Innumerable times, like every other Canario too – just because you have them on your doorstop, doesn't mean you pay them less attention than a cobweb on a lampshade. Sure, we go into the dunes time and again to play at Bedouins. It's fun, makes you happy, and even after the hundredth time a dune landscape like this is still impressive.

However, they are shrinking year on year, and it is quite possible they will soon be gone or at least won't exist in their current form any more. They certainly won't in a few million years, but the timescale stated by the experts is much shorter – they talk of the next 100 years. That's what happens to natural treasures that are forced to their knees at the hands of humankind. You scrape off a bit of the dunes here and there, and then bam, they are gone.

There are plans to carry out reclaiming of the dunes. After all, what is Gran Canaria without the dunes of Maspalomas? No one here really wants to imagine that. However, those who have read attentively and can still remember: in the chapter about Playa de Las Canteras (see ch. 50) we spoke about an isthmus in the northeast covered in dunes.

Within only a few decades these were levelled to the ground. So it's a miracle that these dunes here still exist. And now? Head off into the dunes before they disappear! And don't forget the selfie, which will barely be possible, as the dunes are so full of selfie-takers, aka Smombies. *¡Sonreír!*

Address Dunas de Maspalomas, 35100 Maspalomas, San Bartolomé de Tirajana | Getting there Southeast of Maspalomas, panorama view including a dune information centre behind Hotel Riu Palace at 84 Paseo Costa Canaria | Tip The Faro, in other words the lighthouse, the Charca, i.e. the pond, and the Playa, the beach, are usually mentioned in the same breath as the dunes of Maspalomas. Playa del Inglés and Paseo Marítimo also belong to that same list. Sometimes the 'vile' classics also have to play their part.

69__The Colossal Volcanic Basin

Round the rim or down inside, both ways satisfied

One of the major geological and landscape highlights near the capital is this colossal volcanic basin. It is almost 250 metres deep, around 1,000 metres in diameter and has a circumference of almost three kilometres. This has always been a great destination for a day trip. It is never the same, always different.

There are a multitude of volcanic basins spread across the whole island. After all, back then the island spat out lava from the interior of the earth at a fiery rate, comparable only with fighter pilots activating their ejector seats. But the Caldera de Bandama has something special about it. Something that is indescribable, something that simply has to be felt. You can say what you like about it, but only by being there can you feel the magic of the place and slip into an almost supernatural state of being. On one side, there is the Pico de Bandama, an almost 600-metre-high viewpoint, from which you can spot the tennis courts, and on the other the Caldera de Bandama itself, which can be walked around or climbed into or out of. There is a hamlet on the junction on the GC-802 to the viewpoint, from where a hiking trail leads down into the basin. The hiking circuit forks off from the first left curve of the Carretera de Bandama.

Belief can move mountains, but also leaves behind craters. Here the crater, which was created around 5,000 years ago and has continued to erupt on occasion since then, plays the lead role. The last eruption is said to have taken place almost 2,000 years ago. By the way, the name Bandama is derived from Daniel Van Damme, who was a large landowner here in the 16th century and cultivated vines. And no, this gentleman is probably not an ancestor of 'The Muscles from Brussels' alias Jean-Claude Van Damme – the 'Universal Soldier's' surname is actually Van Varenberg.

Address Monumento Natural de Bandama with Pico de Bandama and Caldera de Bandama, 35307 El Raso, Santa Brígida | Getting there From the GC-800 via the GC-4 onto the GC-802, continue on the GC-802 towards Bandama | Tip There are two vineyards in the area that are worth a visit: one very close by, in the hamlet of El Raso, Bodega Hoyos de Bandama, and the other in a northerly direction, on the junction to the GC-821, Bodegón Vandama.

70_The House of Wine

Local wine, not just for local people

Vines have been cultivated on Gran Canaria from as early as the 16th century. Some historians date the beginnings of vinification on the island even earlier. The indisputable fact is: grapes are trodden and refined here today at the highest of standards. As already mentioned in 'The Vibrant Vines' (see ch. 32), the current winemaking generation is passionate about upholding the standard in the internationally recognised wine-growing area of Gran Canaria. One may marvel in astonishment, but there is still unused wine-growing land and there is still some scope for new vineyards on the field maps and the land-use plans.

The volume of production is measly in contrast to the world's larger producers, but that is often precisely where the key to the matter lies. Bigger and lots, and always more and more – these kinds of capitalist slogans should have long since been consigned to the dustbin of history. Seen through rose-tinted spectacles, the vineyards on Gran Canaria are all creative-artistic wine producers, who create sensual drops of joy and pleasure in humble harmony with the vibrant vine. As the Scottish novelist and travel writer Robert Louis Stevenson memorably said, 'Wine is bottled poetry.'

The refurbished time-honoured building La Casa del Vino, which includes a wine museum, tasting room and restaurant, in which only wine from Gran Canaria is served, is an ideal place to treat yourself to the whole of Gran Canaria in a goblet. But always take it easy and take it slowly; after all, you don't want to trample all over the bouquet before it has even had a chance to develop.

Based very loosely on Plato, wine is a gift of the gods out of mercy for humankind. I wouldn't go quite that far, although to disagree with someone like Plato certainly demands the possession of cojones. Let's put it this way, in the style of Schiller: a glass of wine can deify devils.

Address Casa Museo del Vino, 26 Calle Calvo Sotelo, 35300 Santa Brígida, +34 928 644484 | Getting there From the GC-15, turn right onto the gravel-covered area before the junction with the GC-320 | Hours Museum: Tue–Fri & Sun 10am–2pm; restaurant: Tue & Thu 1–11pm, Wed 1–6pm, Fri & Sat 1–11.30pm, Sun 1–4pm | Tip Right next door is Mercadillo de Santa Brígida, which is a typical Canarian market, and Finca El Galeón, which offers several walking paths through a natural landscape, some well maintained, others less so, as well as some animal enclosures, planted areas and a small water museum.

71_The Oldest Golf Club

Where the British first swung their clubs

Everyone knows the long-running Volkswagen Golf series, named after the traditional sport of hitting balls into holes on accurately cut lawns. Poppycock! It was neither the sport, nor a sea bay that gave its name to this stalwart of the compact automobile landscape. It was, in fact, named after the Gulf Stream by a VW employee in Hannover. But here, at this venerable club, there are no misunderstandings. Here the focus is golf, the sport of golf, which is of British, or more precisely Scottish heritage. Although it has recently been proven that Holland is actually the country in which golf originated.

The British footprint on Gran Canaria is, as we already know, immense. In the 19th century, the island was a geostrategic piece of land of priceless value. It was the British especially who flexed their muscles over the island and were its secret rulers. The British were also responsible for bringing many kinds of sport to Gran Canaria, primarily football, whose origin also does not lie in England, even if it continues to be seen as the motherland of football. It's like the story of pizza and Italy. But try telling the chef at your local Italian, Trattoria such and such. BAH! He would certainly have a thing or two to say about that and may resort to spitting on your pizza.

Golf gained in popularity in 1891 with the construction of the first and still the oldest golf club in Spain. But not among the wider public, as entry into the club was reserved initially to the British or a selected handful of Canarios. Now everyone, member or not, can carry their clubs along the fairway. It's a 5,000-metre, 18-hole, par 71-course, with driving range, putting and pitching green. All of which is built into hilly terrain, thus making it highly challenging.

But the sport still isn't everyone's cup of tea. The majority of people prefer sports with slightly bigger balls.

Address Real Club de Golf, 12 Lugar Campo de Golf, 35300 Santa Brígida, Las Palmas, +34 609 062944, www.rcgolflaspalmas.com | Getting there From the GC-802 onto Camino a La Caldera to the club | Tip You can hit a slightly larger ball back and forth on the club's tennis court on the edge of a volcanic crater. Grand slam tennis! *¡Rimbombante!*

72_The Pottery Workshop

All clay is not the same

Pottery making and the firing of clay and minerals was once a very big thing on Gran Canaria, and a hot one too of course. Even the island's first defilers, nonsense, colonisers – I wouldn't want to confuse this with Edward Lee's Cthulhu Mythos novel – were active potters. Pottery making is one of the oldest human handicraft techniques, with its beginnings in the Palaeolithic era. The oldest ceramic finds are a good 30,000 years old. Now very much niche, ceramics and earthenware have always played a large role.

Who else, if not the British, who run through this book as a common thread, owing solely to their past and partly suffocating presence on the island, had the earthenware of this ceramics stronghold shipped back home by the shed-full. The potteries of La Atalaya, together with those of the Lugarejo settlement, were the best addresses on the island for ceramics for decades. They extracted their best clay from a nearby slope, which can no longer be harvested as the area was declared building land, despite much resistance, and a whole village was built on top of it.

The potteries were renovated in the spring of 2018. They mainly produce commissioned work. But a series of artists also use the rooms as pottery ateliers. In addition, there is a small pottery shop and an exhibition space. And in the neighbouring building the cave dwelling of the most famous potter of Atalaya, Francisco Rodriguez Santana alias 'Panchito', who learned the traditional techniques from his mother, has been converted into a museum.

Earth, water and fire, that's all that is needed. And of course the corresponding hands, which are a central element in creating its shape.

You aren't thinking of the pottery scene from the 1990 film *Ghost*, accompanied by the evergreen 'Unchained Melody', are you? For many people, pottery really is a burning passion.

Address Centro Locero de La Atalaya, 11 Camino de la Picota, 35307 La Atalaya, Santa Brígida | Getting there From the GC-80 onto Calle el Ramal, continue on Calle Cura Navarro to Camino de la Picota | Hours Mon–Fri 10am–2pm | Tip In the western part of the village is the Parroquia del Santo Cristo de La Misericordia de Valdepenas, a house of god and one of almost a hundred on the whole island.

73_The Stubborn Dragon

To fall or not to fall, that is the question

Santa Brígida was the first municipality on the island that began keeping a tree catalogue in 2008 for listing singular trees. There are seven in total at the moment. One of them is the Drago de Pino Santo, or dragon tree – a wonderful specimen, that literally makes jaws drop due to its striking position. It is known right across the island, even though most people have never even set eyes on it.

A tree like any other, the philistine might think, but the astute will appreciate the distinctiveness of this dragon tree. By the way, I have yet to come across any selfies with this dragon online, but it is only a question of time. Dragon selfie! Cool!

This dragon doesn't need taming. On the edge of a crag, half hanging out, and leaning more than Pisa's famous tower, it is hard for the simple minded among us to understand how it can support itself in such a position. I therefore have no explanation for you. This specimen is a wild one, that is, a dragon tree that wasn't planted by human hands.

Its powerful trunk grows directly out of the cliff, it is an impressive 17 metres tall, and its crown has a diameter of 13 metres. The majority of us may not be dragon tree specialists, but I have been told on good authority that these dimensions are not surpassed by any other dragon on Gran Canaria. Until some tiquismiquis, as nitpickers are called in Spanish, comes along and finds one that beats it by an acorn.

Forget it, the Drago de Pino Santo is a hit no matter what. And he's a vigorous fella too. According to experts, this dragon tree is over 250 years old and is in the best of health. No one has seen it breathe fire yet, but red blood is said to flow through its veins (actually, it's a reddish resin secreted by the bark and leaves). In fact, there are numerous legends about the blood of the dragon. But don't get any funny ideas about cutting into it!

Address El Drago de Pino Santo, GC-151, s/n, 35309 Santa Brígida | **Getting there** From the GC-15 onto the GC-151 towards Los Silos. After Los Silos, before the bend at the bridge, follow the path on the left after the bus stop. After almost 200 metres the dragon rises up on a cliff on the left side. | **Tip** Further on the GC-151 towards the west is La Bodega de La Montaña, where you'll find down-to-earth cooking for hungry bellies.

74_The Crumbling Castle

A thoroughbred castle, stone for stone

It is astonishing how some buildings go to the dogs, left to rot and crumble away. Sadly, it is the cursed fate that currently befalls this whimsical castle. You may rub your eyes, but it has now been unused for quite a while, and there also seems to be little movement on this front on the horizon. Seen from the outside, it is a majestic monument and painterly muse. No Neuschwanstein, no Dover Castle, no Kenilworth Castle and also no fairy-tale Cinderella castle, but an eye-catcher driven into decline, that has earned more than the current ravages of time.

From the outside, you can glimpse a view or two into the courtyard and sense the regal and lofty ambience that springs from the walls and rooms. There are as yet no weeds forcing their way out of the ground. Nature has not yet taken possession of the castle, but it won't take long before the process of natural renaturation takes command. The only way to reach the inner realm of the castle would be to use a captive bolt pistol. Quite impractical for most of us. After all, who carries a pneumatic bolt pistol à la Anton Chigurh, alias Javier Bardem, around with them?

The castle is a good 60 years old and was once run as Museo Castillo de La Fortaleza el Hao, which processed the municipality's archaeological finds. There is a restaurant connected to the back of the castle that apparently has direct access to it. There is a rumour that there is a connection from the restaurant to the castle – something like a hidden door that you find in a James Bond movie.

As it is often the case with such buildings, when the right people press the right buttons, abracadabra, the castle will open again. Of course, there are always plans to reopen the museum or use the castle for events and things like that. So keep your ears open, as it is unlikely that the castle, which is owned by the family, will stay closed for ever.

Address Museo Castillo de La Fortaleza el Hao, 2 Calle Juan del Río, 35280 Santa Lucía de Tirajana | Getting there Right on the GC-65, on the right on the way into the village, on the corner of the GC-553 | Tip The village offers, in a pattern repeated in dozens of others on the island, a plaza, a parque and an iglesia. It's an ensemble that is to be found in every casco, old town. Nevertheless, this trio radiates a very individual charm in each town or village. Motivate yourself for a short walk through the old town.

75__The Irrepressible Eyrie

Fortress, hideout, shelter or temple?

According to the newest appraisals of the archaeologists who are examining this pre-hispanic Guanches site, it is a bit of all of those things, and especially the mythical 'Humiaga' temple of the indigenous people of Tamarán. No, I'm not talking about the esteemed planet of the Vega planetary system Tamaran from the DC universe – the accent on the third 'a' is the clue – but rather the name that the natives gave to the island. So next time you're at the travel agents, just tell them you want to fly to Tamarán. But be very careful about accenting that 'a', otherwise you may end up landing among a bunch of superheroes or villains.

And where does the irrepressible eyrie fit into all of this? When the Spanish philanthropists took over the island in an altruistic manner at the end of the 15th century – this might not be the right place to talk bluntly about ethnic cleansing and the slave trade after all – the last remaining Guanches are thought to have retreated to the eyrie, which is today known as La Fortaleza de Ansite, although the 'de Ansite' is now considered wrong. The true rulers of the island rebelled unyieldingly against their displacement, enslavement and their death.

It was nothing but a whistle in the wind, as the conciliatory, orthodox, pious Conquistadores were resolute in their actions. The only choice left to the few remaining indigenous peoples, in order to avoid falling into the hands of the Conquistadores, was suicide. And so, according to lore, the very last Guanches to still breathe in freedom threw themselves from the eyrie, crying out 'Atis Tirma' ('for my land'). Phew, heavy stuff!

From an archaeological point of view, however, a very exciting place that served religious acts including animal sacrifices. The bones of goats were found inside an organised cave complex from the 6th century. *¡Increíble! ¡Una sensación!*

Address La Fortaleza (de Ansite), GC-651, s/n, 35280 Santa Lucía de Tirajana | Getting there From the GC-550 onto the GC-651, then follow it to the end | Tip Beforehand, on the GC-651 after 2 kilometres at 48 Calle Hoya del Rábano, is the Centro de Interpretación de La Fortaleza. It's a classic interpretation centre where you can find out more exciting information about the irrepressible eyrie.

76 Mirador El Guriete

A view in sight is always welcome

On a volcanic island that rises up out of the sea, mountainous and not flat, on which there's one gorge after another and one massif nestles into the next, there are stunning panoramas to be spotted every few metres. And so, especially in the 1990s, when tourism on Gran Canaria was really buzzing and booming and the island blossomed (to death), one mirador, i.e. viewpoint, after the other was modelled into the landscape.

Sure, you would chug across the island and stop every few metres to capture highly meaningful snapshots of intoxicating views. This, of course, impedes the traffic and is moreover also (mortally) dangerous. Countless photo-hungry tourists ended up accidentally – so not like the Guanches of La Fortaleza (see ch. 75) – falling down cliffs.

It soon became clear: the island needed easily accessible and safe viewing platforms. This platform here is long in the tooth and is visited less frequently than many others today on Gran Canaria. An island – or should I say 'tourist island'? (or better still 'dream island'?) – which has a holiday-making clientele, can't keep abreast of everything of course. The maintenance of the constantly growing number of 'attractions' is difficult, if not impossible. Are they keeping everything in a pristine condition? No, that's just the way it's presented in the catalogue.

Mirador El Guriete is one of the steep kind, with a gravel car park, clifftop path and round brickwork platform. And it not only offers a vista, but also an opportune view through gorges and crests, typical for Gran Canaria, and yet this time with a certain extra. The view really is magnificent, but why not find out for yourself? Back in the day it was a really hip place, although now it's a bit shabby round the edges. But no fear, it's good enough for a safe selfie. You don't necessarily have to do a handstand on the railing. Say CHEESE!

Address Mirador El Guriete, GC-65, between 12 and 13 kilometres, 35280 Santa Lucía de Tirajana | **Tip** Southeast, within striking and smelling distance is a typical Canarian granja, as livestock operations and farms are called in Spanish. This granja is specialised in the breeding and use of goats. They do not accept groups of visitors, but you can approach the outdoor enclosures without causing any problems.

77__The Palm Reservoir

A Canarian phoenix without wings

On the Canary Islands, our endemic date palm is the *Phoenix canariensis*, which is seen as the natural symbol of the archipelago and has palm leaves in place of wings. In fact, the palm has nothing to do with that wondrous and mythical bird, the phoenix, in its scientific name. This, according to Hesiod, can grow almost a solar year old and burns in its nest that is ignited by the sun, in order to then rise from the ashes as a worm, which changes into an egg, out of which it hatches as a rejuvenated phoenix. What wonderful imagination! But it does have something to do with Tamara.

Better said támara, which derives from Aramaic and means date palm. Or also támbara, into which an innocent 'b' has sneaked. This is what the fruit of the Canary Island date palm is called, serving birds in particular as nourishment. I mean birds with wings and not 'strange' birds on two legs, as the latter generally prefer eating African and Arabian dates. The Canary Island tám(b)ara is not edible, at least they are neither marketed, nor do you see people hanging on the Phoenixes picking them.

The reservoir, finally filled again after many years – it rained in spring 2018 after a long dry period, even in otherwise rain-free zones of the island, and many thirsty reservoirs filled up – offers a thrilling mountain backdrop and is surrounded by a charming palm grove. However, the trace of time is clear to see on the trees, and compared with the hundreds, or even thousands of palms that still stood 10, even 15 years ago, there are not many left today. Reservoir plus palm grove was once a big deal, when everything still thrived abundantly: it was one of the island's most popular postcard motifs. But you can still breathe in the glory of former times. The reservoir separates the two municipalities San Bartolomé and Santa Lucía de Tirajana, and was completed in 1974. *¡Que cosa más bonita!*

Address Presa de la Sorrueda, Embalse de Tirajana, Palmeral de la Sorrueda, Mirador de la Sorrueda, GC-651, s/n, 35280 La Sorrueda, Santa Lucía de Tirajana | Getting there From the GC-550 onto the GC-651, follow the signs | Tip El Alpendre de Felix restaurant, with its pretty terrace and chic interior, is right on the GC-651 and also functions as a fruit, vegetable and souvenir shop. Breads and pastries are baked in an ancient stone oven. *¡Manjares exquisitos!*

78_The Saltworks

Scoop, scoop then bottle it up

A saltworks has already crossed our path in Arucas (see ch. 26): an abandoned saltworks in a lunar landscape complete with a little saltworks house and some anglers perched between the cliffs. That was a pretty cool place, wasn't it?

And now we come to one of the few saltworks on Gran Canaria that is still in operation and that currently produces the most salt. Some years ago it was derelict, and no one cared a jot about it, until a sociocultural project was initiated in order to finally change that. A resurrection of the saltworks was the goal, along with the vision of rescuing a traditional career from extinction and once again giving Canarian salt, but in particular a horde of young people who had never even heard of a saltworks, a perspective. Salt? Doesn't it grow on trees?

Without further ado, a saltworks master apprenticeship was launched. Around 30 apprentices learned the traditional craft over two years and subsequently assumed the running and upkeep of the saltworks. Since then salt has once again been scooped in earnest, and the young men can pursue a respectable career that guarantees they have enough dough for their daily bread to go with the seemingly endless supply of salt. Instead of picking, they now have to work with the salt stick – not to be confused with a salt lick – but they have long since mastered the technique and a good portion of the training class now really does earn their living with the white gold. Salt, not cocaine!

This saltworks is the only one that packs and labels its own fine and coarse salt. But there is a lack of good commercialisation as well as of serious marketing. There is a consensus there to bring all of the remaining active saltworks on Gran Canaria back into decent shape and to get the salt out into the world in larger quantities by means of a cooperative. A salty business! *¡Una pizca de sal!*

Address Las Salinas Tenefé, Avenida Punta Tenese, s/n, 35119 Pozo Izquierdo, Santa Lucía de Tirajana | Getting there Via the GC-1 onto the GC-194, in Pozo Izquierdo right towards the surfing centre, left to the technology institute. The freely accessible saltworks are on the coast on the left. | Tip Once again the Guanches have something to say here, as tombs were discovered just around the corner, the so-called Túmulos de Tenefé, some of which are rectangular, distinguishing them from most of the other finds on the island.

79__Surfing Mecca

Racing across the sea on the wind

Those who regularly surf, and I don't mean on the internet, can't have avoided hearing about Pozo Izquierdo (El Arenal). Its status as an insider tip has long since exploded. As one of the best windsurfing spots in the world it quite rightly flies the flag and is an absolute must for all surfers. Since 1988, every year this place has been the main showplace of the PWA windsurfing world championship. And yes, Philip Köster, previously mentioned together with Playa de Vargas (see ch. 14) has already pocketed victory in the wave riding discipline here several times.

If you mention Pozo Izquierdo, you must also utter Iballa and Daida Ruano Moreno in the same breath. The twin sisters are Gran Canaria surfers and enjoy international fame and appreciation. For almost 20 years, the two of them have fought out the world champion title in the wave riding discipline between themselves. The 'Moreno Twins' have their roots right in Pozo Izquierdo, where they still live today, helping to shape the surfing scene.

The two of them aren't big celebrities, as you might have assumed, in Spain, or even on Gran Canaria. Here and everywhere else in the world, windsurfing is ultimately a niche sport dominated by men. When the two of them began winning titles 20 years ago, the inequality was even greater, but even a few years ago, when they had already walked off with multiple trophies, it was still hard for them to find new sponsors. Gender equality in sport is going to take a while yet. Full speed ahead!

The area is rounded off by the international windsurfing centre, lots of surfing shops and surf schools, but also a section of beach for bathing. The village is well visited all through the year, and in the summer months the population multiplies. Even those who have little or no affinity to windsurfing can appreciate the magical, beguiling windy ambience that reigns here.

Address 35119 Pozo Izquierdo, Santa Lucía de Tirajana | Getting there Via the GC-1 onto the GC-194 to the village | Tip If you drive northwards through the village and out the other side on Avenida las Gaviotas, and park at the gravel car park on the right before the curve to the left, you can continue on foot to Punta Gaviota, a coastal cliff in the shadow of a wind turbine park not far from Cementerio Vecindario. Close your eyes and breathe in the sea air!

80_The Cheese House

Saying cheese! With a view to boot!

The fact that a lot of exquisite cheese is produced on the Canary Islands cannot have escaped anyone's attention. And it really doesn't matter if you have already visited the cheese dairy I introduced in Agüimes (see ch. 11) or if you have been cheating by skipping chapters and have discovered the cheese factory in Valsequillo (see ch. 106). Did you know that Gran Canaria is the most cheese-mad island of the archipelago? On no other island is there more cheese produced and consumed. But Gran Canaria is also the number one worldwide, if you look at per-head consumption. Now that's a thing, isn't it?

Cheese! Who invented it? Of course it was us Canarios! No, it probably wasn't quite like that. But yes, we Canarios are proud of our cheese, and that's no lie. And in almost every municipality there are first-class cheese producers, but especially in Santa María de Guía, whose cheeses continue to pick up prizes at international cheese events. Gran Canaria truly is a cheese (el)dorado. Oh, to be a mouse!

This simple cheese house was built some years ago in the small village of Montaña Alta with the intention of creating a cheese heaven for visitors. You can try your way steadily through several types of cheese, enter a production room and visit a small museum area. There are three products with protected designation of origin on the Canary Islands, one of them, and the only one on Gran Canaria, is the DOP (Denominación de Origen) Queso de Flor de Guía, Queso de Media Flor de Guía and Queso de Guía.

If you come up from the north via the GC-70, you will often want to stop, as the landscape and views in this part of the island are superb. East of the cheese house there are one hundred and twenty-three steps – or did I miscount them? – up between you and Mirador de Montaña Alta. What a view! And on a clear day you can even see the Teide.

¡Y eso si que es und maravilla!

Address La Casa del Queso, 14 Calle Hoya de la Prensa, 35457 Montaña Alta, Santa María de Guía | **Getting there** From the GC-2 onto the GC-70, in the village turn right towards Bascamao, follow the signs | **Hours** Tue–Thu, Sat & Sun 10am–2pm | **Tip** Spoiled for choice: Iglesia de San José de Montaña Alta southwest of the cheese house right in the village or Piedra de Molino, also right in the village southwest of the church, which serves typical traditional fare.

81_The Chess Plaza

Chess is like football, just without the rackets

Whereas Lukas Podolski represents the view that football is like chess, just without the dice. The words were put into his mouth by Jan Böhmermann, who stole them from Mark Förster, a German poet born in 1972, who has penned such phrases as 'Nothing is as it seems, and sometimes everything seems to be nothing', 'Use time before it uses you' and 'Everyone deceives themselves as well as they can'.

Leo Tolstoy felt sorry for everyone who didn't know the game of chess, as, to his mind, it brings even the learner joy, and leads the expert to great pleasure. Woody Allen was of the opinion that he was too small for the school chess team, and Arthur Schopenhauer thought that the game of chess surpassed all other games, at least as far as the Chimborazo is taller than a heap of manure.

Garry Kasparov saw chess not only as a game with intellectual appeal, but also one that teaches logic, fantasy, self-discipline and resolve. Whereas Albert Einstein represented the view that chess is the quickest game in the world, because you have to accommodate thousands of thoughts every second. Raymond Chandler took a very different line, seeing chess as the most complicated waste of human intelligence to be found outside of an ad agency.

And Anatoly Karpov represented the opinion that he did not have his own chess style and that chess is everything: art, science and sport. Although he suffered a crushing defeat against his constant adversary Garry Kasparov – still the grand master with the best Elo rating after Magnus Carlsen – at the legendary tournament on Gran Canaria in 1996 and ended the tournament without a victory (hitherto a novelty for him), this plaza was named after him.

Those who feel like playing a game of chess, knock yourself out, but I can only advise all players: nip things in the bud if you are serious about chess – and question your choice of opponent. *¡Jaque mate!*

Address Plaza Anatoli Karpow, Calle Médico Estévez, s/n, 35450 Santa María de Guía | **Getting there** Right on Plaza Grande opposite Plaza Luján Pérez | **Tip** Just next door is Guía's sacred treasure, the baroque and neo-classical church, which houses valuable art by the most famous Gran Canaria sculptor, José Luján Pérez. PS: If you want to join in with the game, you'll have to bring the chess pieces with you. *¡Una sonrisa puede con todo!*

82_The Forgotten Guest Villa

Where a famous musical romantic once dwelt

Have you heard of, or more precisely, heard the 'Carnival of the Animals'? To talk of a true instrumental masterpiece is not in my power, especially because the composer himself saw it merely as a musical frippery that he wrote in a playfully comic mood. He never agreed to publishing it during his lifetime. What happened to the composition after he died is, however, music history. Incidentally, the statement that there is good and bad music, and the rest is a question of fashion or convention also came from the composer himself. So who are we talking about?

Correct, the talented Mr Ripley, *¡naranjas!*, the French composer Camille Saint-Saëns, who remained a bachelor for a long time, married a 19-year-old at age 40, begot children, was secretly homosexual, composed heaps of music, gained worldwide fame and held court on Gran Canaria up to seven times. You didn't see that coming, did you? Yes, yes, the great man was on Gran Canaria more often than most of us. He even has several streets named after him. Nobody here can pronounce his name, especially the second surname.

What exactly he did on the island, please don't understand it suggestively, is not completely handed down. His stays were limited to the end of the 19th and the start of the 20th century. At this time, it was not uncommon for well-heeled gentlemen to visit the island and, how shall we put it, enjoy holidays. But in the frequency with which good old Camille visited? An affair you say? Well, there can be no limits to your fantasy on that one.

What is certain, however, is that Camille shared a preference for male ballet dancers with Pyotr Ilyich Tchaikovsky – which even went so far, that, during a visit Camille made to Pyotr's, they performed an 'impromptu pas de deux', in which Pyotr embodied Pygmalion and Camille was Galatea – and that when on Gran Canaria, he always lodged in the Villa Melpómene.

Address Villa Melpómene, Carretera Variante de Silva, s/n, 35450 Santa María de Guía | **Getting there** From the GC-2 Agaeta towards Las Palmas onto the GC-70, first exit on the roundabout, sharp right, right after the underpass, red house with green painted window frame on the left | **Tip** South of Camino Llanos de Parra you will find yourself in a sea of bananas. If you follow the path to the end, you'll reach the coast. By the way, the talented Gran Canarian author Santiago Gil went on the trail of Camille and wrote the fictional novel with a connection to reality, *Villa Melpómene*. It's worth reading! PS: The exclamation *¡naranjas!* means 'rubbish'!

83__The Intricate Jeweller's Shop

And the intricate haberdasher integrates in time

The sewing needle and I are a really bad combination. Last time I tried to mend my trousers, I ended up having to buy new ones. Haberdashery just doesn't suit me. So there's no comparison with Mrs Haberdashery herself, the creative and shrewd seamstress Cruci, who has been nimbly realising her customers' wildest clothing dreams here since for ever and three Big Bangs. She has been making unique masterpieces for years now.

Her speciality is traditional clothing, which is worn especially at the Romerías, the church fairs. There's a Romería somewhere on the island almost weekly, and in the meantime some, er, most of them are hyped like lactose, gluten or histamine. All a load of mumbo jumbo and they generally end up as mass drinking orgies. And just like Oktoberfest or other regional commercial 'parties', it has become fashionable to dress traditionally. Good for Cruci, as making the dresses is what bakes her daily bread (or at least brings in the dough), although she also has fashionable clothes in her range, beautiful one-offs conjured up by her symphony of fingers.

Her neighbour Fati in the parallel street makes fashionable jewellery and design collections and individual pieces with exuberant originality and unique style. This is jewellery in all its glory and in every imaginable facet. Chains, rings, bands in various materials for every possible body part, developed from the only true source: inspiration.

You can't see the jeweller's shop for all the jewellery and you can't see the haberdasher for all the haberdashery. No, that wouldn't be possible, although you will be thrilled by the two intricate setups and their inspirational and creative owners. But the shops are small and cosy, so it's quite easy to keep an overview. Then again, you might lose the overview of your wallet, as there are many great things on offer.

Address Mercería y Ropas Típicas Cruci, 19 Calle Marqués del Muni, 35450 Santa María de Guía; Las Minuencias de Fati, 3 Calle Médico Estevez, 35450 Santa María de Guía | Getting there From the GC-292 onto Calle Médico Estévez, right at Plaza Grande, right into Calle Marqués del Muní; from the GC-292 onto Calle Médico Estévez | Hours Cruci: Mon–Fri 9am–1.15pm & 5–8.30pm, Sat 9am–2pm; Fati: Mon–Fri 10am–1pm & 5–8pm, Sat 10am–1pm | Tip Not far off at number 31 Calle Pérez Galdós you can buy Queso Flor and at number 40 there are handmade pastries. And in case you need some fruit, you can get that at number 51.

84_A Window onto the Sea

And the coolest kickabout on the island

The north coast of Gran Canaria contrasts so greatly with the south coast that there is neither a rational nor an emotional reason to compare the two, never mind wanting to throw them together in the same pot. On the contrary, their chalk and cheese difference makes us realise the yellow-red shiny diversity this island offers up to our hearts, which long for delicate and affirmative distinction. Nourishing our hearts, we whisper sweet nothings along the glorious coast, let the wind blow our cares and wrinkles into the open ocean and accept the lightly winged breeze of the sunny side of life in inimitable spirit, while we hug each other through the window to the sea, and feel ourselves ensnared and embraced by it. And then, bang, we get a football straight to the head. Did that really just happen? *¡Pues sí!*

The village of Caleta de Arriba may be a sleepy hollow, but there is a crumbling picturesque stucco window to the sea here and the coolest place for a kickabout on the island. When I was there, a few children were kicking it 'like Beckham' or better 'like Silva' – David Silva is currently the most successful footballer from Gran Canaria – and the father of one, several or all the children was functioning as a wild gesticulating trainer on the edge of the pitch.

I asked if it would be okay if I took a couple of photos. *'Claro que sí, sin nigún problema, pero tendrás que jugar con nosotros entonces'*, came the answer, which basically meant that I could take photos, but only if I joined in afterwards. No sooner said than done! And so we ended up playing football for a good hour in the scorching heat, the father always energetic with tactical instructions. And when I was completely worn out, the kids could only offer me commiserative smiles. Fortunately, it was lunchtime! So we all went home to Doña Nana, who had cooked a delicious meal of old clothes!

Address Mirador del Pescador, 2 Calle Pizarral, 35469 Caleta de Arriba, Santa María de Guía | **Getting there** From the GC-2 onto the GC-294, after La Atalaya signs to Caleta Arriba, at the roundabout right at the start of the village | **Tip** There are a dozen old fishing huts at the foot of the cliffs at the end of Calle La Ballena to marvel at. You reach the beach via Avenida Virgen del Mar. PS: Doña Nana isn't a restaurant, but rather the mother of the father, who, by the way, was only the dad of two of the seven dwarves. And Snow White? Incidentally, 'old clothes' was the name of the dish: ropa vieja.

85_The Cliffhanger Cross

At the end of the world, the bell rings ding dong

Beating a path to the Cruz de La Campana de Toscón was once only for the bravest and boldest. Today there are railings around the 'Roque Vivo', on which this original ensemble, made up of campanile, bronze bell, altar and cross, stands. You can of course still do the cliffhanger, but it would only be for the gallery.

This beautiful sacred place was built by the villagers themselves in several stages from the middle of the 20th century. There is no other ensemble on Gran Canaria like this one here, captivating with its unusual design and formidable location on the cliff edge. And yes, it is quite a long way out in the middle of nowhere, virtually at the end of the island, and yet right in the middle.

In the centre of the cross, behind glass, is a silver Jesus of reduced size, and at its base is a niche with the image of the Sacred Heart of Jesus. The bell is made of bronze and bears the original inscription 'Leon y Castillo'. Where exactly it comes from is not completely clear, but it must be well over 100 years old. It is suspected that the bell belonged to a steamship, indeed to the first named 'Leon y Castillo', which was built in 1888 and that ran aground off Gran Canaria in 1910. The ship could not be saved, but it was emptied before being left to its fate. Some priest must have purchased the bell somewhere years later or found it and gifted it to the village of Toscón.

A popular local story says that the morning after a villager, who was considered a witch, died, the bell was found to be guarded by two crows, there to prevent the old witch coming back to life, flying around on a broomstick and causing mischief.

You will certainly come across droves of crows on the one-lane road that leads to El Toscón and twists and turns largely without crash barriers. There are also plenty of cyclists and motorcyclists. So take care!

Address Cruz del Toscón, Mirador El Toscón, 87 Barrio el Toscón, 35368 El Toscón de Tejeda | **Getting there** From the GC-60 onto the GC-606, after 5 kilometres | **Tip** Go ahead and ring the bell. In the past, this was only basically done on one of two occasions – either within the framework of holy mass or when a villager had died. However, knowledgeable visitors ring the bell, as ringing it three times in a row is supposed to bring good luck. Further west on the GC-606 is Mirador de Siberio.

86 The Legendary Pine

I'll burn the devil out of you, my child!

The several-hundred-year-old pine watches over the reservoir with composure and hides a tragic and appalling secret. The fire-branded shadow in the trunk of the tree of the beautiful young Casandra, who was oh so in love with her Carlos, Antonio or Javier, who was killed by her jealous father in an indescribably gruesome manner, bears witness to a long-past atrocity that still burns on into today and tomorrow. Casandra made a Mephistophelian pact, in order to take revenge on her father, but he got to her first. He chained her to the pine and burned her to death right in front of her own family and the whole village. It's said that her screams through the blazing fire can still be heard today on some dreadful nights. Blood-curdling stuff indeed!

The Pino de Casandra is one of the oldest trees on Gran Canaria and was always watched eagle-eyed during the course of the building of the reservoir in the 1930s and later in the course of the further hydraulic development in the 1950s, and meticulous care is taken that it remains intact.

This pine is indeed a singular tree of the very finest character, that can't just be felled. And the place in which it stands is as if it were made especially for it.

The pine is a good 20 metres tall, at around 4 metres it splits into two large arms, and the crown has a circumference of a good 5 metres. The almost annual fires (sadly often triggered by human hand, mostly intentionally; how atrocious!) have yet to bring the tree to its knees, but have left some branding marks on it. Scars shape the character but fire has ultimately only made this pine stronger.

The tree was long known as 'El Pino Bonito', i.e. the pretty pine, and was only renamed after the incident with Casandra. Despite all the legends, it isn't cursed, so you can touch it without hesitation. But you'd better be gentle! People say you get a hex if you're rude.

Address Pino de Casandra, Presa de las Niñas, 35368 Tejeda | Getting there GC-605 after 10 kilometres, opposite Área Recreativa Presa de las Niñas; if the reservoir is full, as it is at the moment, walk around the outside | Tip Every Canario knows this area and was probably here at least once a year with their whole family as a child and later with their own children, for barbecues and tapas. The same goes for me. So take a full picnic basket with you. Westwards on the GC-605 is the Mirador de Inagua.

87_The Sturdy Monolith

A cloud rock, a toad and a monk

Which would seem not to go together at all at first, and yet this trio is one of the most popular hiking destinations on the island. The volcanic chimney, the Roque Nublo (cloud rock), together with its associated little brother, the Roque Rana (frog), is one of the most emblematic symbols of the island, and an ancient place of worship. Furthermore, the Roque Fraile (monk) greets us from a couple of hundred metres away. And there it is, a trio, which couldn't have been better if you'd made it up.

The cloud rock is depicted on countless postcards, advertising brochures and travel platforms – the biggest volcanic monolith in the world can even be seen from many places on the island. But being there live and in person is a completely different thing. I walk, wander or trail run at least once a year on the rocky plateau, most recently at sunset. To stand up there on the really flat summit, a good 1,800 metres up, next to these 80-metre-tall basalt breccia giants, with imperial views and blissful thermals, is to feast on moments of pure life and the revelation of your own existence par excellence.

In 1932, three Germans climbed the 80-metre giants for the first time. The climbing route is still there today – it is the one on the right, where a corner protrudes half way up. They commissioned the island's best blacksmith in Gáldar to forge the pitons, and these have yet to fracture or lose their grip. The Roque Nublo is extremely popular among Gran Canarian climbers and there are several routes with different levels of difficulty. I have already been on the giants three times, a good friend of mine 44 times. *¡Fanfarrón!* In the middle of the plateau there are two medium-sized stones, which are arranged diagonally around 10 metres apart. The point half way between these two stones is the geographic centre of Gran Canaria. Indulge! *¡Un día es un día!*

Address Roque Nublo, 35299 Tejeda | Getting there GC-600, after 48 kilometres, car park La Goleta, hiking route signposted, around 30 minutes | Tip Coming from the north on the GC-150 is the Degollada Becerra lookout point, which presents views of the Roque Nublo and the Roque Bentayga. PS: A slightly longer hiking route that leads into the car park of Goleta begins in Llanos de la Pez, Las Mesas.

88_Texeda Brewery

One beer, two beers, three beers and a piglet

Canarian beer? Sure, of course it's a thing! To talk of craft beer being a trend would be a bit last year. Hand-crafted beer is now as common as sliced (artisan, sourdough, gluten-free) bread. But on Gran Canaria it is quite rare. Texeda, which is simultaneously a microbrewery and restaurant, brews the highest beer in the Canary Islands and serves it up in chic 0.33-litre bottles. Here, at a good 1,000 metres above sea level, they turn out three varieties: a classic ale, an almond-flavoured ale and a Scottish export 80.

The high-quality water comes from a nearby natural spring, Roque Nublo, so virtually *kilómetro cero*, as they say around here. Yes, you guessed it, 'kilometre zero', which means pretty much the same as locally sourced, in other words, no long transportation footprint and the product is not only regional, but comes from within a close radius around the place of production. A philosophy that is also applied in the kitchen. Currently around 80 per cent of the foodstuffs used is kilómetro cero, around 30 per cent is even home-produced.

A slowly but steadily growing farm including vegetable gardens and fruit trees, all organically and ecologically cultivated, which they will also show you around on request, also belongs to the brewery-restaurant ensemble. They currently keep various breeds of chicken and goats, and pigs are on their way soon. Currently the locally sourced pigs are butchered by the head chef himself, but in the near future they wish to build up their own herd of the protected breed 'Cochino Negro de Canarias'.

The still young, yet experienced, Borja Marrero, the Gran Canarian owner and hardworking master chef and his team, have successfully served up modern Canarian fusion cuisine in a laid-back ambience paired with their fresh home-brewed beers since opening in 2017. That's unique on Gran Canaria. *¡Estupendo!*

Address Cerveza Texeda, 25 Calle los Almendros, 35360 Tejeda, +34 928 666677 | Getting there Directly on the GC-60 in the southern end of the village Tejeda, opposite the petrol station | Hours Tue–Sun noon–5.30pm | Tip Tejeda is the only village on the Canary Islands so far that has managed to secure a place on the official and popular list of Spain's prettiest villages. Why don't you see for yourself! Depending on the season it can get really overcrowded, but not everything can be off the beaten track and in no man's land!

89_Barrio San Francisco

Long hidden, now a hot topic

The quarter in the city of Telde doesn't have very much in common with the Californian metropolis of San Francisco. They only really share the name of Saint Francis of Assisi, the founder of the Franciscan Order, who has also given his name to a multitude of cities and quarters in Central and South America.

Telde is not only the oldest city on Gran Canaria, dating back to the time of the Guanches in the middle of the 14th century, but it was also the first capital of the island. So it's not surprising that the city just oozes history. The historical artistic quarter of San Francisco is one of its gems, yet it has long been under lock and key, in other words, it wasn't marketed. Now these days are over, and it has become one of the island's most well-known secrets, at least in terms of emblematic city quarters. But then, that's how it goes with insider tips in the current era of digital unmasking – they are anything but secret. So instead of an insider tip, we should really talk of an unmasking tip.

The quarter is small, consisting of only a handful of streets. In the middle is a square with a centenarian. It doesn't have two legs, but it does have a thick trunk. It's a magnificent bay tree that all of us would immediately plant in our garden, assuming you have one and, of course, that it is large enough. It would take a numbskull to grudgingly suggest otherwise. Five roads lead off from the square in a star shape, which are all connected by the bordering outer streets.

You will find the so-called 'monteras' on one of the roads that leads away from the 100-year-old. They are neither hats nor glass roofs, but rather step-like terraces, which were used in the past to save ladies from touching their servants when mounting their horse. Such a function has become obsolete today – now it is at the very most chic classic cars that are mounted here.

Address Barrio San Francisco, 35200 Telde | **Getting there** For example between 37 and 42 Calle León y Castillo on foot turn into Calle Fray Juan de Matos, continue on Calle Carlos e Navarro and Calle Tres Casas to the bay tree | **Tip** The city quarter of San Juán is the neighbour to the east and is basically the bigger, more famous brother that long held San Francisco in its shadow. For a long time it was the case that the bourgeoisie lived in San Juán and Jewish residents and artists were to be found in San Francisco. Between the two quarters is Casa-Museo de León y Castillo at 43–45 Calle León y Castillo.

90 The Colourful Tutti Frutti

All bar ice cream, striptease and chin-chin

Those who stray onto the beach and coast of Ojos de Garza, generally really have strayed off the beaten track. Except, and this really is the only exception, if someone has given them an unmasking tip (see ch. 89). Playa de Ojos de Garza is the first beach north of the airport. From here you can see many birds whoosh past, but most of them have fixed wings and two engines. And maybe the odd colourful old bird, like Mr Peñita, but more on him in a bit. It is mostly the back end of aeroplanes you get to see here, as they mainly make their initial climbs rather than approaches here. But this does nothing to cancel out the noise level.

The small coastal quarter is made up of two parts. One part stretches along the beach and is, apart from the beach, a collection of around 100 houses pressed tightly together, a few twisting alleyways and a road that ends in a cul-de-sac with a chance to turn round. The other part is south of the beach and is the realm of the aforementioned Mr Peñita, a 73-year-old jack of all trades, who many, many years ago began, on a whim, to collect everything that the sea waves washed up on his shores, and to find a use for it.

Over the years, a colourful tutti frutti has been formed, that seems quite wild but is in fact an impressive and unparalleled omnium-gatherum. Over the years many other things that he found goodness knows where have been added. He calls it recycling. Others call it art. He doesn't throw anything away, instead finding the right place for everything.

The large piece of land and the building complex are very convoluted and partially inhabited. And if Mr Peñita doesn't happen to be taking his protracted siesta, he's happy to guide anyone who's interested through his realm. Entry permitted!

Address La Casa Peñita, Playa Ojos de Garza, Avenida Juan Perez Betancor, s/n, 35219 Ojos de Garza, Telde | Getting there From the GC-1 onto the GC-140 to the coast | Tip At the north end of the quarter, the restaurant Zurita awaits to serve you freshly caught fish on a welcoming terrace. Extremely popular among locals.

91 The Crazy Lizard Terrace

Help, socorro, the lizards are loose!

And on we go with the superlatives. Gran Canaria is home to the endemic Gran Canaria giant lizard, the largest species of Canary Islands lizard. The lizards, which have grey skin and a pale belly, can grow to a length of 80 centimetres. In the past, however, this was far from being the end of the story, as fossils of the beast have been found measuring one-and-a-half metres. There are related giant lizard populations on the other islands, especially on El Hierro and La Gomera, but these specimens are generally no longer than 40 centimetres. People on Gran Canaria insist they have the biggest specimens, and are determined to have the designation 'Giant of the Archipelagos' protected.

Here, on the small inlet of the maritime coastal promenade with the three benches, also called 'La Terraza de Los Gigantes' among those in the know, that is 'the terrace of the giants', the scaly lizards scamper as if in the throes of dancing mania over the rocky ground to the sea and crawl hastily between the rocks, as soon as you lean over the railings or move too suddenly. But if you approach the whole thing carefully and walk to the railings in slow motion, turning your attention downward without turning your head, you can witness the colourful social life and tireless efficiency of the reptiles. Don't be surprised if you catch sight of not just a few, but in fact dozens of lizards.

Among locals it is known as the crazy lizard terrace, and they themselves are in large part responsible for one of the island's biggest lizard populations establishing itself here. They feed the lizards with kitchen scraps and provide them with fresh water. But there are others who aren't quite as lizard-friendly and enjoy letting their dogs loose on them. Most of the time, however, the dogs come out of the whole thing empty pawed. These lizards can be aggressive and give you a very nasty nip.

Address La Terraza de Los Gigantes, Paseo Marítimo de la Garita, s/n, 35212 Telde | Getting there North of Playa Hoya del Pozo, just after the hill | Tip Playa Hoya del Pozo and especially Playa del Hombre beyond it are popular among surfers. Yes, the coast of Telde is dotted with beaches. And there are two more to follow (see ch. 99).

92 The Falcon Mushroom Gorge

Pull up your socks and keep your eyes peeled!

All around the world the climate is currently changing in an undeniable and unprecedented way, at least according to some. Others claim that this is madness and counterclaim that all this climate scaremongering is a huge piece of fake news. No matter who is telling the 'truth', over the first months of 2018 the clouds over Gran Canaria provided record rainfall. By the start of March the dams had collected over 12 million cubic metres of water, guaranteeing agricultural irrigation for the whole year.

The water keeps on coming. This is also true for Barranco de Los Cernícalos, one of the few glens that carry water all year round. The Barranco is also home to the island's largest falcon population. So, stretch a bit, limber up, lace up your shoes nice and tight and strap a rucksack onto your back – off we go through meadow and scrub, up hill and down dale in the walking rhythm of the miller, to several waterfalls. You will even be able to marvel at a double waterfall. The route is intended for everyone, but should always be walked with care. Known among locals for decades, it has also been discovered in recent years by visitors who are looking for some contrast to the beach. And for some mushrooms! The zone is considered mushroom-dorado. Yes, I'm sure one or two among you might hunt out a few suede boletes; horns of plenty; pig's, hare's and jelly ears; milk caps and slimy spike-caps; or monk's head in the woods back home. But on Gran Canaria? Yes, of course there are mushrooms on Gran Canaria.

About 700 species are recognised, although a rough estimate of what is actually out there suggests over 1,000. A good two dozen are edible, while a handful are poisonous. In a cesta llena de setas canarias, a basket of Canarian mushrooms, you might find ceps, chanterelles, milk-caps and oyster mushrooms. *¡Que rico!*

Address Barranco de Los Cernícalos, GC-132, s/n, 35211 Lomo Magullo, Telde | **Getting there** On the GC-132 follow signs, after Merenderos de Los Cernícalos, GC-132, 66, continue straight on, rather than following the GC-132. The path leads cross country into the gorge, partially signposted, mainly recognisable. | **Tip** Not exactly round the corner, but at Bar Yazmina, (44 Calle Maestro Nacional, 35215 Telde) they serve one of the best bocadillos de pata, the famous Canarian black pig's trotter sandwich, on the island. It is not uncommon for people to stock up with sandwiches here before heading off into the barranco.

93 The False Geyser

They say it's the island breathing

Snakes and ladders isn't really that popular on Gran Canaria. Locals prefer card games such as 'el envite' or 'la zanga'. Nonetheless, it is of course possible to experience the highs and lows, in quick succession, here too. In this case, it is thanks to a geological coastal formation that is typical for volcanic islands and that has been assigned the Canarian neologism 'bufadero' – a blowhole. These are costal cavities connected to the sea by holes in the style of a roof hatch. When the waves flood the jagged hollow from the side and from below, the air and the water are shot out of the roof hatch and a multitude of other small openings. This creates a hearty whoosh, the so-called 'bufido'.

The whole thing resembles a geyser, although what is going on here is not volcanic in origin and has nothing to do with hot springs. But the hole in the rock does offer you the possibility to throw yourself in for a trip in this water elevator. This sport is very popular among the young. Although it is not without its dangers – a few scrapes and bruises are certainly to be expected – jump boldly into the bufadero and let yourself be pulled down a few metres by the movement of the sea, before then being catapulted up into the air with the next wave. This natural phenomenon is an attraction particularly in the summer months, and people gather around the false geyser in droves. There are only a few of these bufaderos spread around the whole island, the one in Mogán (see ch. 58) is also called a bufadero, but it is more of a sea grotto, which neither whooshes nor elevates.

Bufaderos arise on volcanic islands when streams of lava flow into the sea. The cooled surface of the lava flow solidifies, but liquid lava continues to flow underneath. Lava tubes and other cavities are formed. Over time, parts of these collapse, and ta-dah, you have a bufadero.

Address El Bufadero de La Garita, Paseo Marítimo de la Garita, s/n, 35212 Hoya del Pozuelo, Telde | Getting there From the GC-1 via the GC-10 into the GC-116 to Hoya del Pozuelo. Right onto Calle Salvia after the roundabout from Calle Tomillo, then left onto Calle Fagonia and continue on Calle Romero. At the end, cross the promenade opposite the car park. The bufadero is in the middle of the rocks. | Tip Playa de Hoya del Pozo to the south is seen among locals as the prettiest beach on the coast of Telde. It's all a matter of taste of course, so check it out for yourself. ¡Para gustos están los colores!

94_The Four Doors

Exemplary sculptural cave architecture

You certainly can't accuse this place of massaging its ego. On the contrary, places like this have been pushed ever further into the background and are left to their own devices, even if they were once among the most well-known attractions. It's a fate that many places suffer on an island that has had to continuously pull new magnet locations, in other words highlights and sensational attractions, from up its sleeve or out of the hat for decades.

While one forgets that Gran Canaria is so extremely rich in big attractions, new locations are pinned on the map at an alarming rate. But what happens to those that are long in the tooth? What happens to the fragile, wrinkled seniors, that have turned a bit ragged around the edges? They are largely left to their own fate and crumble away. High-flyers like this one degenerate into slow movers, and no one does a thing to stop them from becoming forgotten. Yet no one has a bad conscience.

Sure, the occasional coach tour or two still drops by here, and you even find this place on new maps and via the relevant channels, but that doesn't hide the fact that it has been branded boring. A fatal mistake, especially considering that the site dates back over 500 years, and many Guanches would turn in their graves.

One could describe the style of this jubilant cave ensemble as pre-Gaudí. That's Gaudí, as in the one-of-a-kind world-famous Spanish architect, not gaudy! In the northern part, the eponymous gates, in the southern part winding living and column caves and above an almogaren, i.e. a sacred gathering place where libations were made to the gods. The whole site is accessible, and you don't need to be an archaeologist to feel a shiver down your spine just being here. This isn't just architecture without a plan, this is accomplished art realised by archaic means and tools. *¡Una verdadera proeza!*

Address Cuatro Puertas, 35215 Cuatro Puertas, Telde | **Getting there** From the GC-1 via the GC-140 onto the GC-100, after the roundabout left into Calle Guanche to the dirt track, then continue upwards on foot | **Tip** Further south on the GC-100 in Ingenio is the Museo de Piedra y Artesanía (1 Calle Camino Real de Gando). Museum? Well, yes, it's more of a dusty hodgepodge in the style of an antiques flea market. And the stones? A private collection from dead patrons, mainly made up of stones from Africa.

95_The Iron Dragon Tree

Roundabout-crazy Canarios in a sensual orgy

The Canarios and their roundabouts: it's love at first sight. And an inexhaustible love at that. What has been and continues to be built here on Gran Canaria roundabouts may well be record-breaking. Who needs traffic lights if you can have roundabouts? One might almost think that it's a little bit over the top that they build roundabouts here like shopping centres are built elsewhere. Although the Canarios, as we already know (see ch. 47), are pretty keen on those too.

But it isn't just about creating traffic junctions. For years, a downright roundabout competition between the municipalities has broken out. In the sense of the classic 'Who has the longest?', the question here is 'Who has the prettiest?'

So the roundabouts are cared for and decorated all year round or to fit the season. Of course, a roundabout, as a colourful green area or similar, is just asking to be flaunted. But here on the island it has become a kind of silent competition, and it is often accompanied by bags of taxpayer money, which really doesn't sit well with the population at large.

This specimen, which should fittingly represent all of the island's roundabouts, is the largest artistic work on the middle island of a roundabout on the island of Gran Canaria. A 22-metre-tall symbolic iron dragon tree weighing almost 500 tonnes. Only recently it was furnished with a new ground surface as part of a general course of beautification of all roundabouts in the municipality of Telde. Previously grass, it is now sand and red-coloured charcoal. Apparently it suits the sculpture better!

This monumental island symbol was designed and built in the long-forgotten times of the year 2002 by the artist Sergio Gil Socorro and it cost around a cool million euros. Peanuts for an artwork of such cachet, right? Most people still can't help holding their heads in their hands. *¡Derroche!*

Address La Rotonda de El Dragon de La Garita, GC-116 and GC-10, s/n, 35212 La Garita, Telde | Getting there Roundabout at GC-10 and GC-116 | Tip If you drive on the GC-10 to La Garita and follow the smell of the sea, you'll finally reach Playa La Garita. PS: Those who take a selfie with both this dragon as well as with the stubborn one (see ch. 73), will turn into a dragon themselves – and a fire-breathing dragon at that. ¡La leche! All joking aside, I'll pay for a round and then some for the first double selfie taker!

96_The Olive Finca

Olives as draught horse, batteries as horse power

When you think of Spain, it's hard not to think of olives. All right, the gastronomic classic is probably sangria, but that really is very 1990s and for most associated with hordes of sun-burned tourists from Northern Europe, legless and out of control on Mallorca. Anyway, you won't catch anyone Spanish drinking it, never mind the Canarios. The culinary delicacies paella and tortilla? Yes, these can be delicious, depending on how they are prepared, but you have to be lucky. But Canarian olives – they are simply amazing. Although the olive tree is a bottomless pit, i.e. a water-greedy Goliath, there are a huge number of them on Gran Canaria. Many Canarios name one or in fact several of them their own, and use their very own family brine recipe in order to cure the raw drupe and remove some of the bitter substances, turning them into healthy power packs full of oleuropein and oleocanthal. No, that's got nothing to do with Chantal!

There are more than a handful of olive trees on this finca, which produces small quantities of olive oil, generally sold straight from the farm, and prepares olives for consumption following traditional recipes. Everything is ecologically and organically cultivated and processed.

But the finca is not only a production site. It also offers a whole arsenal of additional attractions, for example a small zoo with birds and animals, a greenhouse, a shooting gallery, agricultural theme park and a children's play area. And not forgetting the go-kart course with battery-powered karts, inaugurated in 2018. Opened to school classes and tourist coach trips for a few years, now after an extensive revitalisation of the whole site, it is now open to occasional customers too.

You may well know the famous sunflower painting by Vincent van Gogh, but do you also know the one with olive trees? Go and ask Daddy Bing or Mother Google!

Address Centro Ecológico Cultural Los Olivos, 12 Camino Campo de Volcanes Rosiana, s/n, 35215 Telde, www.centroecologicoculturallosolivos.com | Getting there From the south of Telde, turn off the GC-100 towards Las Medianias, turn left at Calle Rio Sil, then follow the signs | Hours Sun–Fri 10am–5pm | Tip Still in Telde itself, right on the GC-100 at 70 Calle José López Suárez, is Boutique del Pan, which bakes huge quantities of home-made cakes and pastries. How about a trucha canaria or a bollo?

97 The Recuperated Turtles

Recuperation of afflicted sea paddlers

Sea turtles have paddled bright-eyed and bushy-tailed (well, not literally) through the Seven Seas for over a million years, but nowadays they don't have much to smile about. And that, rather unsurprisingly, is all down to humankind.

The pollution of the sea and nesting beaches, combined with an unspeakable greed for their shells, eggs and their meat, has pushed all seven species of sea turtles almost to the edge of extinction. *¡Realmente una locura!*

In the rehabilitation centre for wild animals in Taliarte, which is part of the University of Las Palmas' marine science and technology park, turtles that have fallen victim to human activity in one way or another are looked after. Every day, thousands of plastic bags and other plastic rubbish finds its way into the sea, and Morla's and Crush's fellow turtles mistake the bags for jellyfish and choke on them. For many millions of years only edible things swam or floated in the seas, but nowadays they can often be traps. Artificial traps that capture the tortugas, as turtles are called in Spanish.

In addition to the rehabilitation programme, a turtle breeding programme is also sustained. Here representatives of the loggerhead sea turtle are looked after – they have the byname boba, which means 'silly' in Spanish. Eggs from the Cape Verde Islands are brought here and the brood is reared for around a year, before the turtles are released into the Canary Sea.

If you walk along the side of the building complex inland, you can catch a good glimpse of a handful of small pools containing 'silly' turtles on the right before the roundabout. Most people simply walk past this short section of fence, even if an unusually located wooden bench on lava platforms right in front of it serves as a clue to this turtle curiosity. The spot is called 'turtle love corner' and couples often do a love sit-in here. *¡Salvar las tortugas!*

Address Instituto Canario de Ciencias Marinas, Calle I. Canario de Ciencias Marinas, s/n, 35214 Taliarte, Telde | Getting there From the GC-1 via the GC-18-13 onto the GC-116, third exit on the GC-116 roundabout, at the end of Carretera a Taliarte on the left after the roundabout right at the car park | Hours Viewable from the outside only | Tip The lighthouse of Taliarte towers into the sky a stone's throw away. You can't climb it, unless you decided to do your best King Kong impression, but walking around it opens up wonderful views of the stony coast of the municipality of Telde.

98 The Swimming Route

Streamlined from buoy to buoy

Exploring a section of the coast with a stroll on dry land, perhaps armed with several scoops of ice cream in a cone and plenty of sun cream on your skin, is part of the standard repertoire for every visitor to a coastal region. It is very rare, on the other hand, to do this on water, and by swimming only in very few exceptional cases. Here you will find such an exception, with a swimming route marked out by yellow buoys.

This is the island's first official sea swimming route. It leads from the small fishing village of Taliarte to Playa de Salinetas. And back. Or vice versa. A good 1,000 metres long and at a suitable distance from the coast. The aquatic race 'Travesía a Nado de Salinetas Dolores Álvarez' takes place here every summer – once by night and once by day. The race's popularity has grown year on year and this year the maximum number of participants who will be able to compete is 325. The entry fee for the race is a kilogram of non-perishable foodstuffs, which is donated to the local church parish.

Dolores Álvarez was a real character from Telde and was known all over the island. Born in 1921, she was a woman who was always ahead of her generation. She was the first woman on Gran Canaria to sit at the wheel of a truck, a pioneer in the male-dominated field of clay pigeon shooting, and she wore trousers. Gender equality was in her blood. A viewing platform on the beach of Salinetas is also dedicated to her.

The race is part of the traditional series of summer events 'Súbete a la ola de la vida', which means something along the lines of: 'Surf on the wave of life'. Main points on the programme are the music festivals 'Telde Young Beach Fest' and 'Melenara Guaquete Sun'. The fringe events offer further sporting, musical and cultural activities, as well as various workshops and environmental initiatives. Swim, little fishy, swim!

Address Canal de Aguas Abiertas, 35214 Taliarte, Telde | Getting there From the GC-1 via the GC-18-13 onto the GC-116, second exit on the roundabout with the GC-116 into Calle Luis Morote, straight on to Paseo Marítimo de Taliarte, swimming route begins south of the harbour | Tip Greet Neptune: the Roman deity stands in front of the pier on Playa de Melenara day in, day out, sometimes with one arm or missing prongs, if stormy waves have maltreated him. But within days, at the latest weeks, the missing limbs or prongs are repaired so he's rarely anything but three-pronged!

99_The True Dream Beach

Dancing with the flying lizard's head

Not seeing the beach for the sand. Yes, this is how it sometimes feels on Gran Canaria. There are as many beaches as there are smart phones, smart phonies, phone smarties and foam parties elsewhere. But not all beaches are born equal. You will find any and every kind of beach on the island, but you probably won't have the time to go to all of them. So you will usually end up going to the beaches that are close to your accommodation, or drive intentionally to an unmasking tip. Only the very brave trust in their instinct and discover beaches for themselves. Everything is allowed, everything welcome, each to their own.

And only the best for you. The two beaches that respectively represent the throat and the back of the neck of a flying lizard's head – more on that soon – are the true dream beaches. Sure, *para gustos están los colores* (sound familiar?), there is no accounting for taste, but taste is also no lottery. Taste means laying your cards on the table and nailing your colours to the mast. Playa de Tufia, the throat, is a dream like out of one thousand and one beaches. If you haven't been there, you really don't know what you're missing. And those who try to describe it only rob it of its magic. Playa Aguadulce, the back of the neck, is a textbook example of a bay. In this case even literally, assuming this tome achieves such status. Both beaches lie pretty much back to back and are only a stone's throw from one another.

And now to the flying lizard head, with which both beaches dance, as if they were grimacing St John's Dancers in the light of Magec, the sun. If you take a bird's-eye view, for example with the help of Daddy Bing, the flying lizard head appears like scales falling from your eyes. Can you see it? The head and body were once covered in tomato plantations, which had their heyday on Gran Canaria in the middle of the 20th century.

Address Playa de Tufia and Playa de Aguadulce, 35219 Tufia, Telde | Getting there From the GC-1 onto Carretera a Tufia to the end, to the south is Playa de Tufia, to the north Playa de Aguadulce | Tip Directly on the car park before the village is Mirador Playa de Tufia. Above the village is the Zona Arqueológica Poblado de Tufia. And in the village itself there is, among other things, a mermaid. Both beaches, especially Playa de Tufia, are also an underwater paradise for snorkelling and diving.

100 The Vibrant Promenade

A path for both sports junkies and couch potatoes

This kilometre-long stretch of coast is extremely popular among the locals. In general, there are people out and about here at every hour of the day, many working out, some taking walks, others just chilling out. Others still swear by the romantic nocturnal hours in the light of the moon with the sounds of the waves and the smell of the sea. They generally mean its aphrodisiacal effect. This also finds its carnal expression in certain places. Between Taliarte and Playa del Hombre there is even a kind of unofficial drive-in cinema. The screen is the dark sea, and the film plays out in your head.

Near the La Garita beach, right on the promenade, is a colourful house. It looks like an artist's house at first sight, and even if it doesn't seem very inviting, you may be tempted to try and glimpse a look behind the façade. But be careful, a tramp who isn't quite right in the head lives in this illegal dwelling. He is mostly not there or is asleep, but otherwise he likes to exercise his ample repertoire of Spanish expletives. He has never yet turned physically violent. On the other hand, people in the area say that he is now dead and the authorities have acquired the house. Via the access to the house you can reach the rocky area around it, which is a colourful treasure trove.

You will encounter many cyclists, walkers, dog owners, inline skaters and even horse riders on this route. And every few metres an angler on the rocks. Time will run away from you and seem short, as there is so much to discover. One or two other delicacies have managed to find their way into this book as independent places, but believe me, there are more for you to find on your own. Also, there are up to 10 different beaches along the promenade where, during the summer, plenty of locals spend their time.

So why not play I Spy, keep your eyes open and enjoy the fresh sea air?

Address Paseo Marítimo La Garita a Salinetas, 35212 La Garita, 35214 Salinetas, Telde | **Getting there** Promenade begins at Playa La Garita or Playa Salinetas | **Tip** Between Playa Salinetas and Playa de Melenara near the quarter of Las Clavellinas there is a small rock pool with a rock tableau that can be reached via some steps. This rarity, known as 'Charca Perez', generally only has space for one dreamy loved-up couple.

101_ The Fields of the Blessed

An Elysian estate to fall in love with

Finca de Osorio was once a majorat estate from the 16th century that belonged to the Manrique de Lara family who moved here from the Spanish mainland. It was acquired by the island government in the 1980s. Since then it has been run as a semi-public nature refuge with over 200 hectares of land. The number of visitors is restricted, and access won't be granted without prior reservation. There is a 1,000-square-metre main building, the former finca, which has been converted into a youth hostel and is in active use, a barn, in which cows, horses and chickens are kept, and other agricultural and forestry buildings.

The site has lots of little gems on offer. Every few steps there's a bewitched forest, a romantic garden or a fountain of youth waiting to put you under its spell, and if you let yourself fall, you'll be drawn into a waxy, soft and warm maelstrom, that merges heart and body with body and heart and will elicit from you an animal-like warble. In the following chapter (see ch. 102) I introduce one of these gems separately, although it does in fact merit several.

I went here several times as a child, also in a group, including overnight stays at the youth hostel, and the new generation has also been here too of course. And that's how it is for most Canarios. People go walking and hiking here, take some refreshment with them, enjoy the peace and nature, recuperate from the stress of everyday life and refuel their souls with luscious green.

Five families currently live on and work the estate. Humans play second fiddle here – and rightly so in my opinion. What nature is capable of accomplishing when the smug, narcissistic rogue doesn't stick its nose in too much is magnificent and requires no more words. Words are hollow, only experiencing it for yourself counts.

So, without further ado, off to the fields of the blessed! No excuses to stay in bed!

Address Finca de Osorio, GC-432, s/n, 35339 Teror, +34 928 219229 | Getting there Near Cementerio Velatorio, GC-43 between 8 and 9 kilometres | Hours Daily 9am–5pm, reserve three days in advance | Tip South of the estate is the town of Teror, where masses of people have been regularly brought in for years. The old town is completely set up for and oriented towards these hordes of visitors, and yet it has been able to hold onto a little bit of its charm.

102 The Goblin Gorge

A good-natured goblin, not a pixie

Undaunted, I strode from the back of the main building of the Finca de Osorio past the beautifully chiselled garden. A thicket of crooked branches were about to function as a barbiturate and dampen my resolve. But no, not me! I resolutely wound my way through and was rewarded only a few moments later: the goblin gorge. What a unique sensation of puckish green and damp. Miracles and fantasy are born right here.

I followed the labyrinthine path on autumnal-coloured leaves, although it was spring, through the few hundred metres of the gorge, flanked by gnarled rocks dripping with moss, that seemed to me to be more alive than a team of wild danseuses who show more than they conceal. With suggestive images in my mind, I noticed, step for step, oh my, the ground too is alive. Sprightly, but not tipsy, I implored the troll who was creeping out of the earth not to pull the ground from under my feet. Generously it granted me progress and guided me on through the goblin realm.

At once I became entangled in a saliva soaked spider web, whereupon a gigantic spider approached in mammoth steps with the intention of finishing me off. But as if by magic it was summoned back and shrank to the size of a leaf on a four-leaf clover. What luck! Reaching the end of the gorge, I put my hands to my head. And then to my heart. I even felt a little afraid. But my trousers stayed dry. There, up between the thick roots in a crevice, was a green goblin with long ears, who lit a pipe with a long match.

What a peculiar picture, I thought. But that is how it is down here in the goblin gorge: reality and fantasy blur with one another and become the threads with which dreams are spun. Now spin your own! The small gorge is easy to reach, with an inconspicuous path leading down into it. And once you are there, you'll find yourself in another world. *¡El mundo de los duendes!*

Address Barranquíllo de Los Duendes, Finca de Osorio, GC-432, s/n, 35339 Teror, +34 928 219229 | **Getting there** Near Cementerio Velatorio, GC-43 between 8 and 9 kilometres, behind the main building (youth hostel) follow the footpath to the right of the garden, at the clearing with five wooden benches take the left path at the tree at the front and wind your way through the thicket | **Hours** Daily 9am–5pm, reservations three days in advance | **Tip** Take a walk to Pico de Osorio, towering almost 1,000 metres. The way there is signposted.

103 Área La Laguna

Parilla, barbacoa or in Canarian: asadero

Fire, fire, charcoal, who's the best barbecuer of them all? Or are we talking about grilling? Apparently, there is a difference between the two. Either way, cooking meat on an open fire is now the number one summer sport! Who doesn't like chucking a few sausages or a juicy steak on the barbie? Probably a vegetarian. Not to mention vegans (or myself). But otherwise the world seems to barbecue like it was going out of fashion.

On Gran Canaria the whole happening is called asadero, and more popular than using your own garden, balcony or backyard are the Áreas Recreativas and Merenderos, i.e. picnic and barbecue sites, that are spread all around the island. Many of these spots were created and integrated into recreational areas long before the barbecue fad. These places are lively and enjoy huge popularity, especially at weekends. People are drawn to the fire pits in their droves, and end up spending the whole day there.

Área La Laguna was built in a volcanic crater, in the middle of which is a small lagoon. A further feature is the hippodrome, in which horse races sometimes take place and of which less than a handful still exist on the island. An even younger laurel forest has also been planted here as part of a European project for the reforestation of laurel trees.

The site is spaciously laid out and doesn't only attract locals. On Gran Canaria, family days out including an asadero enjoy great popularity. It is not rare for people to choose one of these áreas in the middle of the island and then to drive there in convoy. No distance is too great. And by now you should know yourself: the island may seem small, but it is in fact huge. It's not uncommon for people to drive a good one and a half hours to a sublime barbecue paradise. Half way across the island with all the kids and grandparents, all for the sake of a barbecue. Amazing! *¡Épico!*

Address Área Recreativa de La Laguna, Calle Párroco Francisco José Hernández, s/n, 35340 Valleseco | Getting there Follow the signs at the junction of the GC-21 and the GC-30, a few hundred metres away | Hours Daily 10.30am–6.30pm | Tip Very few of these places have a kiosk, but this one does. It is currently run by Mari and Paco. Don't miss the best tortilla sandwich in the world! Not only for people like me, who show anything barbecued the cold shoulder. Although I certainly wouldn't say no to a grilled langostino. Dreamy!

104_ The Irrigation Trough

The human channels water, who channels the human?

As we near the end of our Gran Canaria adventure, we come around full circle. We began with contemporary witnesses of the water management of the past (see ch. 6), and now come to a first-class irrigation trough, in which the water is channelled valley-wards and takes us along with it on an exquisite route. Most of these troughs on Gran Canaria have disappeared or no longer carry water. Although those of you who visited Barranco de Los Cernícalos (see ch. 92) may be raising your eyebrows right now. And quite rightly, as such a channel has already crossed your path there, even if only a very small part of it travels overground.

This one here starts very innocuously on the edge of the road, and those who aren't driven by their own curiosity would simply walk on by. Sadly, this is so often the case when humans once again play the arrogant shoulder-shrugger. Are there any investigators left?

However, if you follow the trough around the corner, along thc wall of the house and the fence, your ears will soon begin to twitch. The view alone is delightful. You need to be surefooted, but you certainly don't have to be a Reinhold Messner type. Meandering, the channel leads us to a fork in the path. The path leads down into an untouched valley, and then at some point on hardly discernible paths to a private piece of land.

Upwards is a harder route, but take heart, a natural sculptural tree and a path through wild terrain awaits. And straight on or, rather, following the trough further, leads along and around the hill and then down towards infinity. A panpipe-like waterway with a scent craving for water and life.

The water will lead the way. And the falcons will circle above you on the thermals, eyes peeled for their prey. Take your time, it is neither early nor late, the water is fresh, but its route is not straight. Channelled human!

Address Acequía Oración de Luz, Lugar La Laguna, s/n, 35340 Valleseco | **Getting there** Opposite the southern access to Área Recreativa de La Laguna | **Tip** Not far, on the GC-21 at Cruce de La Laguna, is the restaurant Arcos de La Laguna. Every few weeks the menu is given a different theme, which always brings new impetus to the selection. *¡Que rico que estaba el lomo de atún con salsa de fiel!*

105 The Lanzarote Laundry

On your laundry, get set, go!

Open the washing machine, put your laundry in, select a programme, and after about an hour your clothes smell like a floral spring breeze. Hand washing? That is reserved for special items of clothing or sporadically to pre-wash stubborn stains. That's not the case here in the Lanzarote laundry. Yes, Lanzarote is the sister island, but in this case it's a village on Gran Canaria in the municipality of Valleseco. Admittedly, not many come here to wash their laundry any more. But that is partly because the Lavadero doesn't have running water all year round.

But when the water does flow, you will find the odd elderly granny coming here with her dirty laundry, showing the washing machine at home the red card. Most don't come by foot, however, but by car. Generally, it is the daughter who drives her mama and all the laundry and the necessary utensils here and then picks her up again a while later. Meanwhile, mama puts on her washing apron, washing gloves and washing hat and works through the laundry in stoic silence and joyful serenity.

It is mainly women over the age of 70, who have spent their entire lives mucking in and getting on with it, and who still want to spend their time beneficially, in other words to fill their time with something active. Of course, they all have washing machines and happily use them, but they understand the powerful feeling of having actually done something. There is nothing more cumbersome than a sluggish body, inhabited by a gloomy mind. Without movement, a person perishes.

For most of us it is hard to imagine washing our laundry there, but we can certainly understand it. There are still a couple of these Lavaderos left spread across the whole island. We live in such fast-moving times, that such a communal laundry facility seems like a witness from the distant past, but if we look a little closer, it wasn't so long ago at all.

Address Lavadero de Tierras Blancas, GC-21, s/n, 35340 Lanzarote, Valleseco | Getting there Right after the junction of the GC-214 and the GC-21 | Tip Right at the junction is an opulent stone platform with information board and fascinating views. According to a Gran Canarian story, this is where a prince secretly kissed a lover, who subsequently changed into a frog.

106_The Cheese Factory

The truth is in cheese

All good things come in threes (see ch. 11 and 80). The small salesroom with a cheese cabinet couldn't be much more inconspicuous. It is located on a road parallel to the town's main street, but not exactly in your face. The locals know about the cheese factory and small cheese shop, but passing trade is rare. People seldom stray into the middle of an industrial street block after all.

Cheese has been made here for 40 years. Their speciality is 'queso fresco', which occupies a special place in people's lives on the Canary Islands. It's a sliceable moist cream cheese, that is quite wobbly as it retains a large portion of the whey. Its production is simple, but as is often the case with simple things, the devil is in the detail, so there are huge differences in quality and taste.

Those who think anything of their cheese don't become politicians, journalists or authors; they enter their cheese into the World Cheese Award. In the 2017 edition their cheeses beat thousands of others from all around the world to take gold and bronze. But in the end, prizes are prizes and the eternal battle for medals and trophies is tiring. What really counts is that the impeccably crafted product titillates the palates of the local population.

What is untypical for such a factory sales point is that it sells cheese made by other producers. But that is the case here, and not industrially produced stuff either, but rather cheese from small-scale cheese makers on Fuerteventura, who still produce 'queso artesano' pretty much in the old tradition. You can of course give everything here a try.

Go along the corridor to the right of the shop to the reception. There you will be welcomed and the in-plant cheese sales counter will be opened for you. It is only staffed continuously for a short time in the morning, as that's when most locals come. *¡Pan con queso sabe a beso!*

Address Quesos Flor Valsequillo, 14 Calle Salvia, 35217 Valsequillo | Getting there From the GC-41 onto Calle Vinagrera, then left into Calle Salvia | Hours Mon–Sat 8am–6pm | Tip Right next door at number 18 is Apícola Canarias. A real honey shop that has everything a honey-lover could dream of, except a machine to shrink the kids. Hardly surprising really.

107_Presa de Cuevas Blancas

Deeper, wider and as robust as a tank

Gran Canaria has a huge concentration of dams and reservoirs at various altitudes. Many of them are out of service and are mutating into ruins. Due to low rainfall, most have had little or no water at all in recent years, which, as we already know, changed in the spring of 2018 and 2019 in a way as never before. The rain came, saw and conquered. Even the really big reservoirs started to fill up, some even to half full.

It wasn't quite enough to fill this specimen though, but that there is any at all, after years without water, is a small sensation in itself. The dam is the highest on the island at around 1,700 metres above sea level and the only one that was built in a self-contained valley basin. Furthermore, it is among the stockiest. The visible part towers a good 16 metres into the air, but the foundations reach just as far down into the ground. Even the width of the foundations is substantial at almost 20 metres. And so it is that this stocky dam is, in principle, indestructible, or at least the most stable on the whole archipelago.

Even though it is located directly on the GC-130, it is hidden in the valley basin, where the air is filled with the sweet scent of white thyme, and flanked by pine trees and other stilted giants that cover up our view of it. If you know where it is, however, it is comparatively easy to find it. A dam that, from among all its relatives on the island, has a uniqueness that radiates a power and majesty that doesn't always emanate from such imposing structures.

Located in a barren area, in which green dominates nonetheless, you are faced with an atypical scene for Gran Canaria, even though it would be fair to say that Gran Canaria is precisely that. Green, luscious and burgeoning, especially when the sky has been generous, in the middle of nowhere, far from deckchairs and sandcastles. And all that at 1,700 metres above sea level. *¡Qué bárbaro!*

Address Presa de Cuevas Blancas, GC-130, s/n, 35216 Cazadores, Valsequillo | **Getting there** The GC-130, after 6 kilometres leave the road on foot in a westerly direction, a few hundred metres through wild terrain | **Tip** Further south on the GC-130 is the Caldera de Los Marteles with a viewing platform. This is a volcanic crater with rich vegetation, which is partly used for agriculture.

108 La Montaña Cabreja

Everything passes, views remain

Insight gives way to the prospect of something forbidden. Although access to Mirador de Montaña Cabreja is not officially forbidden, only the last section of the road is barricaded. You won't find it written anywhere that you mustn't climb up on foot, so limber up, take a run up and clamber right up to the top. The last stretch is a piece of cake, and the view from almost 1,000 metres up is infinitely more breathtaking.

Not so long ago there was a restaurant up here that was very popular among Canarios. The special thing about it was the mixture of the phenomenal location and a miraculous chef. But, like all good things, this also came to an end at some point. The building has been abandoned for years and is crumbling into ruins. There are no plans to reopen this public lookout point, which is partly because it has been put to another use in the meantime. Transmission masts, TV antenna and a lattice mast with vertical Yagi UKW antenna have been erected on the summit. Programmes from Radio Tinamar and Radio Charly among others are broadcast from here.

From up here you have a good view of the numerous farmed meadows, whose cultivated produce is sold at the weekend market of Vega de San Mateo. The municipality has always been very rich in water, and the gorges usually carry the substance from which all life arises all year round. And so the municipality has long been known for its luscious green, vibrant pastures and its agricultural produce.

Up here on Montaña Cabreja you are virtually standing in the middle of the municipality and have an overview of pretty much the whole thing. The restaurant has gone, the house is run-down, the car park has been abandoned and the lookout point long forgotten. But the view – that at least remains. As well as the memories. The memories of an unforgettable holiday on Gran Canaria. *¡La reina es la reina!*

Address Mirador de Montaña Cabreja, Calle Las Cabrejas, s/n, 35329 Vega de San Mateo | Getting there From the GC-15 onto the GC-154 to the barricade. From there walk the last part on foot. | Tip Mercadillo Agrícola de San Mateo in Calle Antonio Perera Rivero right in the town of Vega de San Mateo sells the best the region has to offer on Saturdays and Sundays.

109_The Rustic Horse Ranch

To new horizons on a galloping steed

'A horse! A horse! My kingdom for a horse!' as William Shakespeare once wrote. Possibly not quite a kingdom, but here at the Centro Hípico San Mateo, horses certainly take centre stage. A small team of dedicated horse whisperers takes care of up to 30 horses. Some of them are decommissioned, long in the tooth gee-gees, who are allowed to enjoy their retirement here. The ranch has 10,000 square metres at its disposal and is embedded in natural surroundings, reasonably close to the town of Vega de San Mateo.

On weekdays, depending on the season, there might not be much going on, but at the weekend it's really buzzing or, more accurately, neighing, especially in the summer months. Then Hemingway, Estrellita, Bolo and Kaori, as a handful of the horses here are called, go off on riding excursions in the luscious landscape of the surrounding area. And the ponies on the sandy riding ground also get to take part in the action. The horse-loving locals take classic riding lessons here all year round, and there's a riding camp during the summer holidays. The ranch also collaborates with AFTEC, a horse therapy association.

Integrated into the ranch is Guachinche El Novelero, with a sun deck and a hotchpotch interior. There's a restaurant that serves typical dishes from the neighbouring island of Tenerife and offers dance evenings on Saturdays. When it kicks off, hooves and hips swing to live Canarian or even Latin American music. The goat meat dishes are the house speciality, and of course escaldón de gofio is also served, a sort of porridge made from gofio, that usually functions as a side dish. Gofio is pretty much a staple on the Canary Islands and its origins go back to the Guanches. It is a ready-to-eat flour made of roasted maize or other grains. The restaurant has certainly nailed its colours to the mast with the motto: *¡Bueno, bonito y barato!*

Address Centro Hípico San Mateo, Entrada Mirador Montaña de Cabreja, s/n, 35320 Vega de San Mateo | Getting there From the GC-15 onto the GC-154, then left into Caserío Colorados. It's on the left after a few metres. | Hours Tue–Sun 9am–1.30pm & 4.30–7.30pm | Tip In Vega de San Mateo, opposite the chemist's in Calle del Agua, you can buy freshly ground gofio, virtually straight from the farm, or in fact mill. It has a wonderful smell! You must get some! I often get my gofio from here – it's one of the best on the island! Even after weeks, the paper packaging still smells gofio-heavenly. *¡Una delicia!*

110_The Star Hunters

Stars in your eyes, look to the skies

Stargazing is just one of those things: sometimes it's cloudy, sometimes you fall asleep, and ultimately you rarely look up at the sky intentionally at night. But the stars only shine in the dark. This is where these star hunters come in handy. They run the only observatories on the island: 'AstroEduca' in Vega de San Mateo since 1998 and 'AstroTemisas' in Temisas since 2000.

Together with observatories in Hawaii and Chile, the Canary Islands observatories form the golden triangle of astronomy. The most important observatory in the archipelago, with 15 telescopes, is to be found on La Palma. It functions primarily as a research site and went into operation in 1985. On Gran Canaria, the observational activity is less. Very little astronomical research takes place here and collaboration with astronomical authorities is also quite limited. There are rumours that extraterrestrial beings have been observed from Gran Canaria, but that is considered a hoax among experts.

They look up to the skies all year round on Fridays and Saturdays in Temisas. In the winter months from 9 to 11pm, in the summer months beginning an hour later. On Fridays, there is an introduction to astronomy, while Saturdays is dedicated to astrophotography.

There are various packages on offer in Vega, also during the week, but it is astro-hiking that really stands out: a starry night walk, led by an astronomer, at the end of which you also get to look through the telescope. The observatory in Vega is the first located in a town in the archipelago and is sponsored by the municipality. It exclusively serves amateur research and represents an educational institution.

A third star hunter? Bubbletent Canarias! Glamping under the starry Gran Canarian skies in magnificent surroundings with absolutely breathtaking views.

Set off for the stars! And you? First of all, set off for 'my' island!

Address AstroEduca y Centro Astronómico Büro, 46 Avenida Tinamar, 35320 Vega de San Mateo; Observatorio Astronómico de Temisas, 6.5 kilometres along the GC-550, 35280 Temisas | **Getting there** AstroEduca meets at various places arranged beforehand, Observatorium de Temisas directly on the GC-550 at 6.5 kilometres | **Hours** Events usually Tue, Wed & Fri, sometimes also weekends, from 9pm, www.astroeduca.com; Fri & Sat 9–11pm, sometimes also during the week, www.astrotemisas.com | **Tip** AstroEduca have run the first educational observatory in Spain in the grounds of the Meliá Tamarindos hotel in the south since 2002. Initially only for hotel guests, AstroEduca now also offers non-guests the possibility to hunt for celestial bodies from here. Or do you fancy the meteors (see ch. 63)? Or maybe the ducks (see ch. 65)? Hunting fever!

111 The Unpretentious Murals

Artistic tributes to traditional handicrafts

As in many other towns, Vega de San Mateo has plenty of artistic works to admire. Most of them are sculptures, statues, memorials, or murals. All of these works of art blend sympathetically into the cityscape and make it livelier and more diverse, but mostly they receive little attention. The same goes for these two murals, which are easy to find, but seem unspectacular, even to someone seeing them for the first time. They're just a bit too plain to actually stand out.

But there is often beauty hidden in simplicity. The following sentence comes from Giacomo Casanova: 'An object really beautiful ought to seem beautiful to all whose eyes fall upon it: harmony makes beauty and is always closely linked with simplicity.' And yes, those who wallow in the limitlessness of the spectacular, quickly lose sight of what is true, whose seal is simplicity.

One simply walks past these murals and thinks nothing of it. Stop and look at them? No, after all, you haven't found yourself in a museum in front of a painting by Picasso, Goya or Velázquez. The murals do not scream 'look at us!' On the contrary, it seems as though they don't even want to attract our gaze.

But these murals are pieces of art made by local artists and reflect the old way of life. Both radiate an incredible energy, and their simplicity in material and subject matter hide a much larger symbolic power than you might suspect. Two traditional occupations, that of the shepherd and the baker, are paid homage to here, and they are merged into unity with typical surroundings of former times. Colourful and full of atmosphere, the murals speak to us. And if we engage with them for only a few minutes, we get something back, something we would simply throw away if we walked past without paying attention. To be absorbed in thoughts and feelings creates enormous power.

Address Mural aleatorio a los Pastores, Calle Rambla de Constitución, s/n, 35320 Vega de San Mateo; Mural aleatorio a los Panaderos, Calle el Agua, s/n, 35328 Vega de San Mateo | **Getting there** From the GC-15 into Calle Rambla de Constitución, opposite La Fuente de Sal and from the GC-15 onto Calle del Agua, right next to Pan de la Luz bakery | **Tip** On the forecourt of the town hall, next to Iglesia de San Mateo in the middle of the old town, is Kiosco de la Música de la Alameda Santa Ana, a pretty bandstand in neo-Canarian style, in which concerts are performed on particular occasions throughout the year. *¡Ay mi Gran Canaria! ¡Cuidado que me bebo toda tu sangria! ¡Que buenas són tús panaderías! ¡Ay que quiero que te rías!*

1
28
84
30
29
Gáldar
Puerto de
Sardina
82
2
83
81
San Isidro
Santa María de
Guía de
Gran Canaria
32
31
Los Quintanas y
Piso Firme
4
2
Agaete
Bascamao
5
Saucillo
80
3
1
San Pedro
6
Montaña de
Tamadaba
1443 m
El Risco
21
7
Parque Natural
Tamadaba
22
20
Artenara
Moriscos
1772 m
Altavista
1376 m
Los Caserones
Tejeda
39
37
88
36
La Aldea de
San Nicolás
La Solana
85
87

N
0
1.24 mi
Las Coloradas
51
43
44
La Isleta
52
50
56
LAS PALMAS
DE GRAN CANARIA
47
55
45
San
Felipe
61
23
25
26
Bañaderos
San Andrés
2
Cabo Verde
20
Tinocas
49
Cardones
41
Buenlugar
Arucas
Tenoya
Los Rosales
Juan XXIII
Las Torres
Altas
Triana
Moya
27
24
3
53
Firgas
23
57
El Palmital
La Cruz
Tamaraceite
Vegueta
San Fernando
48
60
Lomo Blanco
40
54
El Palmar
31
102
San Cristóbal
Zumacal
101
San Lorenzo
Tafira Baja
104
42
103
Salto del Negro
Teror
46
Tafira
3
4
Valleseco
Marzagán
Santa
Brígida
69
105
1
73
70
71
Lanzarote
72
Valle de Jinámar
La Atalaya
Ariñez
Utiaca
95
100
109
111
108
89
La Garita
93
Las Lagunetas
Vega de San Mateo
Lomitos de Correa
Playa del
Hombre
91
TELDE
97
106
Valsequillo
Playa de
Melenara
98
Valle de Los Nueve
Tenteniguada
Las Medianías
Playa de Salinetas
96
92

38
3
El Hoyo
Montaña de las
Yescas
1490 m
Inagua
86
Chira
Soria
Montaña de Tauro
1225 m
Mogán
Parque
Natural
Pilancones
Cercados de Espino
Puerto de
Mogán
59
La Playa del Cura
Pueblo de Tauro
58
Puerto Rico
Montaña La Data
1
El Salobre
Balito
El Tablero
Patalavaca
Arguineguín
64
Montaña de
la Arena
Santa Águeda
Pasito
Blanco

Pico de las Nieves 1949 m
107
94
Cuatro Puertas
El Goro
99
4
90
Ojos de Garza
12
Guayadeque
1
Marfu
Las Mejías
San Bartolomé de Tirajana
66
33
Ingenio
34
El Burrero
19
Temisas
74
Carrizal
35
18
9
Morro de las Vacas 1433 m
Santa Lucía de Tirajana
110
10
Agüimes
Montaña Los Vélez
62
17
Vargas
Fataga
14
77
75
11
El Sitio de Arriba
76
Cruce de Arinaga
8
13
Arinaga
Tirajana
Cruce de Sardina
15
16
Sardina
Vecindario
Aldea Blanca
El Doctoral
Pozo Izquierdo
79
78
67
Juan Grande
1
Castillo del Romeral
San Fernando
San Agustín
5
63
Playa del Inglés
Maspalomas
68
N
0
1.24 mi

Epilogue

What a wild ride through my home island. All over the place, across field and through gorge, right into the heart of things and nothingness – into the hustle and bustle or off on the lonely path. The diversity that the queen of the Canary Islands shows us is vast, unspeakable, unequalled. All that's missing is the corresponding hit song. I hope I was able to excite your interest in this unimaginably precious and grandiose jewel on an untouched silver-blue stretch of ocean. It was and is clear to me that Gran Canaria has been an ultra popular holiday island for decades, especially because of *sol y playa*, i.e. sun, beach (and sea). But Gran Canaria is so much more, and even these 111 places are just a drop in the ocean: the variety of the outside world forms the wealth of the inner life. A holiday should, primarily, be relaxing and should free your mind (or fill it with new things), so wanting to discover a whole island on your own is possibly a little ambitious. But reading this book from the successful – quite rightly so as it is wonderful – 111 series, has hopefully contributed to fanning the flames of the blazing fire that is Gran Canaria. I wish you an amazing and richly diverse time on 'my' island, with everything that you expect of it. *¡Nos vemos en Gran Canaria!*

Catrin George Ponciano
111 Places along the Algarve That You Shouldn't Miss
ISBN 978-3-7408-0381-0

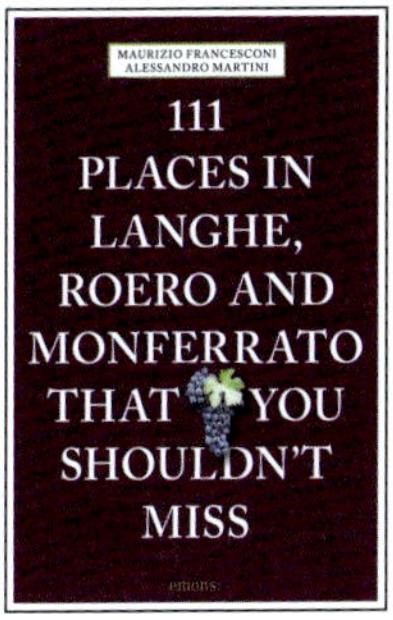

Maurizio Francesconi, Alessandro Martini
111 Places in Langhe, Roero and Monferrato That You Shouldn't Miss
ISBN 978-3-7408-0399-5

Alexia Amvrazi, Diana Farr Louis, Diane Shugart
111 Places in Athens That You Shouldn't Miss
ISBN 978-3-7408-0377-3

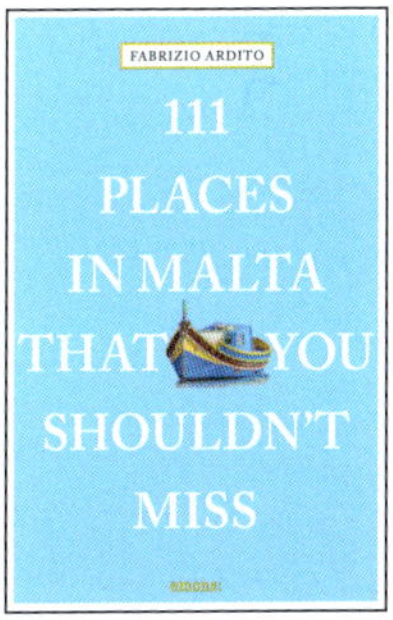

Fabrizio Ardito
111 Places in Malta That You Shouldn't Miss
ISBN 978-3-7408-0261-5

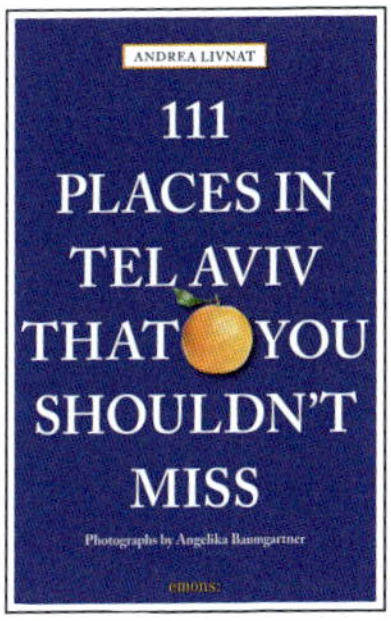

Andrea Livnat, Angelika Baumgartner
111 Places in Tel Aviv That You Shouldn't Miss
ISBN 978-3-7408-0263-9

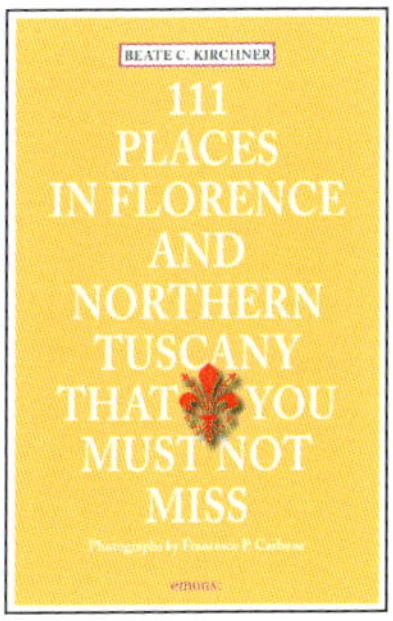

Beate C. Kirchner
111 Places in Florence and Northern Tuscany That You Must Not Miss
ISBN 978-3-95451-613-1

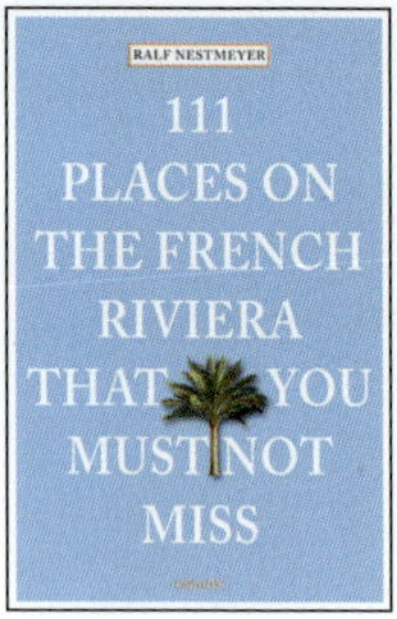

Ralf Nestmeyer
111 Places on the French Riviera That You Must Not Miss
ISBN 978-3-95451-612-4

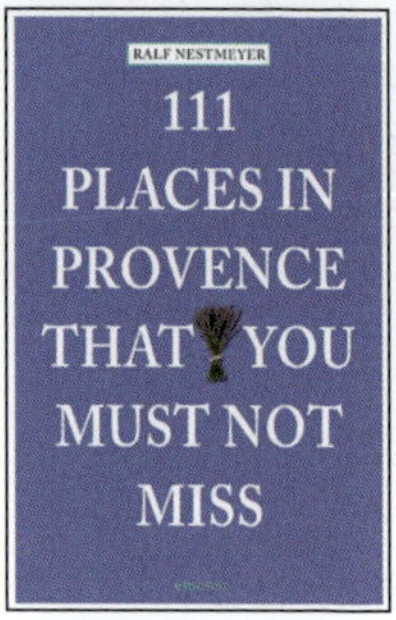

Ralf Nestmeyer
111 Places in Provence That You Must Not Miss
ISBN 978-3-95451-422-9

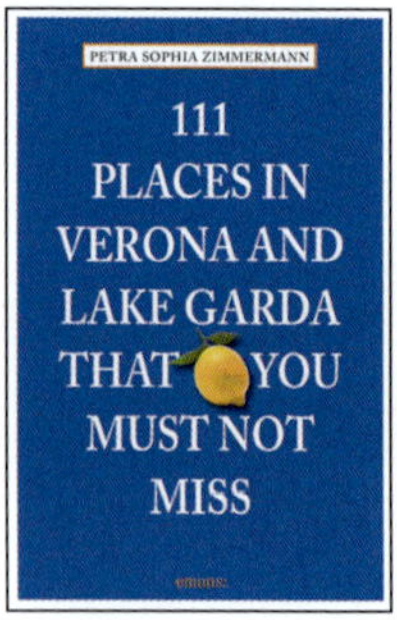

Petra Sophia Zimmermann
111 Places in Verona and Lake Garda That You Must Not Miss
ISBN 978-3-95451-611-7

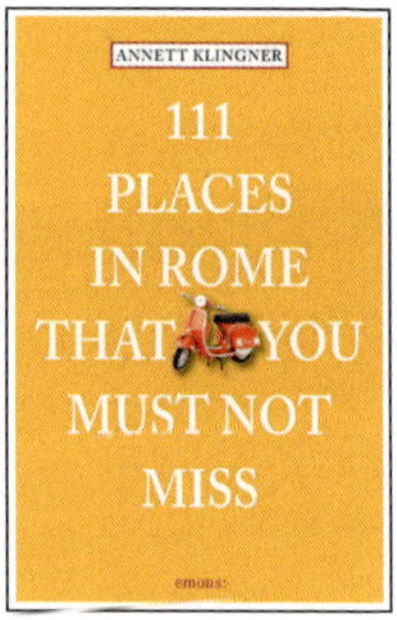

Annett Klingner
111 Places in Rome That You Must Not Miss
ISBN 978-3-95451-469-4

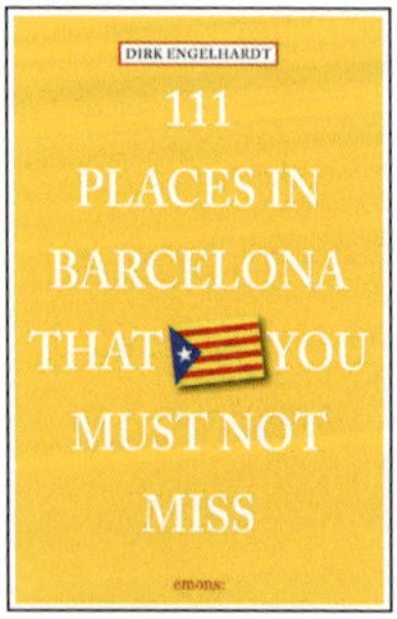

Dirk Engelhardt
111 Places in Barcelona That You Must Not Miss
ISBN 978-3-95451-353-6

Rüdiger Liedtke
111 Places on Mallorca That You Shouldn't Miss
ISBN 978-3-95451-281-2

Kay Walter, Rüdiger Liedtke
111 Places in Brussels
That You Shouldn't Miss
ISBN 978-3-7408-0259-2

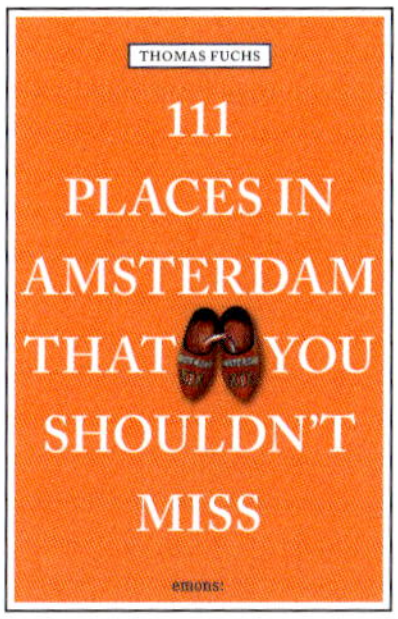

Thomas Fuchs
111 Places in Amsterdam
That You Shouldn't Miss
ISBN 978-3-7408-0023-9

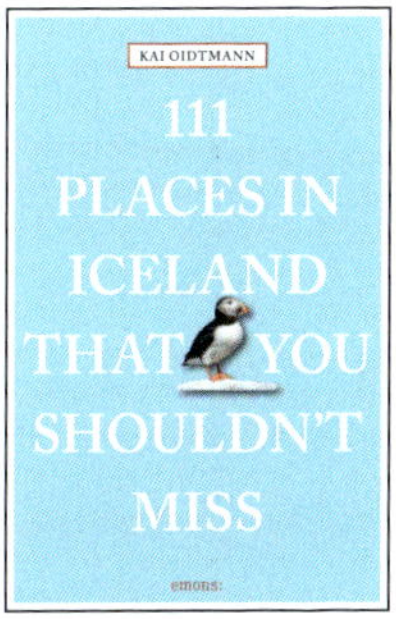

Kai Oidtmann
111 Places in Iceland
That You Shouldn't Miss
ISBN 978-3-7408-0030-7

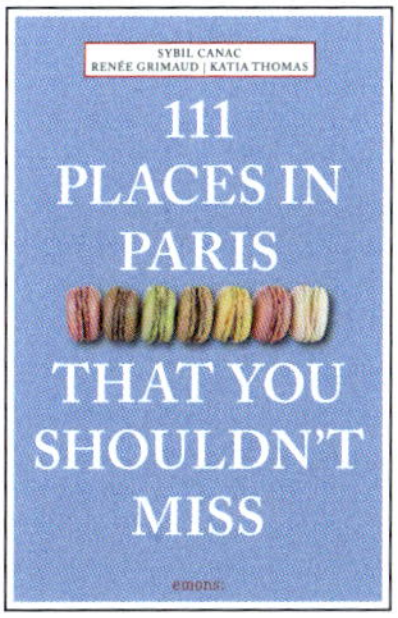

Sybil Canac, Renée Grimaud,
Katia Thomas
111 Places in Paris
That You Shouldn't Miss
ISBN 978-3-7408-0159-5

Rosalind Horton, Sally Simmons,
Guy Snape
111 Places in Cambridge
That You Shouldn't Miss
ISBN 978-3-7408-0147-2

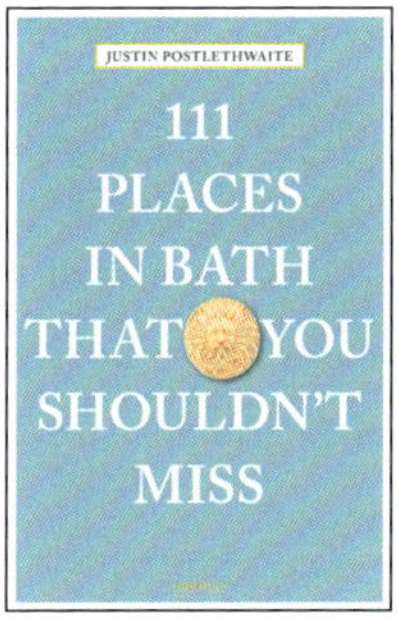

Justin Postlethwaite
111 Places in Bath
That You Shouldn't Miss
ISBN 978-3-7408-0146-5

Acknowledgements

Muchísimas gracias a la maravillosa, valiosa y valiente Saro Arencibia, *al fenómeno excepcional* Antonio Herrera and to the outstanding Emons Verlag team. And of course to my eloquent, liberal and highly constructive editor Vera Nohl.

Este libro nació de la nada para llevarme hacia a ustedes. Ahora todo tiene sentido: SJR y CAJ. No hay palabra que pueda espresar mi tremendo amor por ustedes. Muy cortos se me quedan mis gracias y mis les quiero de nuestro día a día. TCCADMV?

The author

Author **Rolando N. Grumt Suárez**' roots are planted firmly in the earth of Gran Canaria, the island of his birth and his chosen place of residence – he feels at home in every corner of the island. For this book he opens up his personal Gran Canaria treasure chest and looks behind the scenes of one of the most popular holiday islands in the world. High mountain regions, rainforests, palm tree oases, deserts, beaches; a multifaceted island with numerous microclimates that continues to redefine itself year on year. With great joy and skill he has written a topical travel book about what is, in his own opinion, the *isla más bonita del mundo: ¡Disfrute de la reina Gran Canaria!*